はじめに

JN025082

　この教科書は、TOEIC®L&Rテストで500点をめざす学生のために作成したものです。

　本書は、前半部分の文法項目ごとに学習することができる基礎編（Unit 1~8）と、後半部分の語彙やイディオムを中心に学習することができる応用編（Unit 9~12）の二部構成になっています。また、各ユニットでは、PART 5形式の問題に加えて、リーディングセクションとリスニングセクションをそれぞれパート別に扱い、バランスよく学習することができるように構成しています。

　さらに、Unit 13には500点を確実にするための基礎的な問題で構成された基礎力確認テスト、Unit 14には500点以上のスコアをめざす学生のために少し難易度の高い問題も入れた実力テストを収録しています。テストの量的には実際のTOEIC®L&Rテストよりも少ない分量ですが、それぞれに試験時間が設定されていますので、すべてのパートを設定時間内に解く練習ができます。

　また、Unit 15には、補強問題を用意しました。学生が苦手とするパートに焦点を当てることで効率よく学習することができます。

　本書での学習を通して皆さんのスコアが伸び、取得した英語資格によって、さらにさまざまな将来の目標を達成することができることを願っています。

　最後に、本書の企画段階から完成までお世話していただきました松柏社の森有紀子氏と永野啓子氏に感謝の意を表したいと思います。

鈴木　淳・高橋哲徳・高橋史朗・Simon Cooke

本書の使い方と特徴

　本書は学生が無理なく500点を突破できるように、TOEIC®L&Rに頻出する語句を使用しながら、文法項目ごとの基礎的な問題から語彙やイディオムなどの応用問題まで幅広くカバーしています。

　本書はUnit 1からUnit 4まででリスニングのPART 1からPART 4を一通り終えられるように構成されていますので、テキストを最初のユニットから始めることで、基礎編（Unit 8まで）を終える頃にはリスニングセクションでは各パート（PART 1～PART 4）をそれぞれ2回ずつ、またリーディングセクションではPART 6とPART 7を計4回ずつ学習し終えることになります。

　応用編では、語彙問題とイディオム問題を中心に取り上げながら、特殊な表現を含む問題や図表問題、また複数の文書に関する読解問題などを取り上げ、さらなるスコアアップを目指せるようになっています。

基礎編の特徴（＊基礎編にはユニットごとに10分程度の確認テストが用意されています。）

・リスニングの例題に関しては、ディクテーションのための空所を用意しています。

・PART 5形式の例題は2択になっています。練習問題については通常の4択となっています。

・PART 6、PART 7の例題は3択にしていますので、少し易しくなっています。練習問題については通常の4択となっています。

・各ユニットで学習した文法項目の問題はPART 6のなかでも必ず出題されていますので、そこで復習することができます。

・TOEIC®L&Rに頻出する語句を各ユニットの最初の部分で確認できるよう、Word Checkを配しています。

・各ユニットで出てきた重要語句や重要表現は、別に用意された確認テストで復習することができます。その日の授業の終わりや次回の授業の始めなどでお使いください。

応用編の特徴（＊応用編にはユニットごとに10分程度の確認テストが用意されています。）

・語彙やイディオムを中心に学習することで、文法だけでは得点できない部分をカバーし、よりスコアアップを確実にすることができます。

・各ユニットの最初の部分でチェックする語彙やイディオムは、別に用意された確認テストで英文を通して復習することができます。その日の授業の終わりや次回の授業の始めに復習としてお使いください。

・各パートで少し難易度が高い問題も出題していますので、500点以上のスコアをめざすこともできます。

■基礎力確認テスト

　テキストで学習した文法項目や語句の復習をはじめとして、その他にも500点を取得するのに必要な語句や文法項目などを考慮して作成しています。授業で使う際には、たとえば試験時間を40分、解説および板書を50分として授業を行ってください。

■実力テスト

　500点あるいはそれ以上のスコアに必要な語彙やイディオムなども考慮して作成しています。また、全体的に少し難易度を高くした問題も出題しています。授業で使う際には、たとえば試験時間を40分、解説および板書を50分として授業を行ってください。

■補強問題

　学生が苦手とするPARTを重点的に学習できるようにしています。

TOEIC® L&Rとは

TOEIC®L&RとはTest of English for International Communicationの略で、英語によるコミュニケーション能力を評価するテストです。スコアは10～990点までの得点で示されます。すべてマークシート方式で、問題文や指示などはすべて英語でなされます。

TOEIC®L&Rは、リスニング100問（約45分間）、リーディング100問（75分）で構成される試験です。途中に休憩はなく、2時間で200問を解きます。

問題形式について

リスニング

*音声はアメリカ、イギリス、カナダ、オーストラリアの4カ国の発音となっています。
*試験中にメモを取ることは禁止されています。

■PART 1　写真描写問題（6問）

1枚の写真について、4つの英文を聞いて、最も適切な描写をしているものを選びます。問題用紙に英文は印刷されていません。

■PART 2　応答問題（25問）

1つの質問と3つの応答を聞いて、最も適切なものを選びます。問題用紙に英文は印刷されていません。

■PART 3　会話問題（39問）

1つの会話につき3問ずつの設問を解きます。2人あるいは3人の会話と設問を聞いて、選択肢からそれぞれの解答を選びます。図やグラフ、地図などを見て答える問題もあります。会話文自体は問題用紙に印刷されていませんが、設問と選択肢は問題用紙に印刷されています。

■PART 4　説明文問題（30問）

1つの説明文につき3問ずつの設問を解きます。音声で流れるさまざまなタイプのナレーションを聞いて、選択肢からそれぞれの解答を選びます。図やグラフ、地図などを見て答える問題もあります。説明文自体は問題用紙に印刷されていませんが、設問と選択肢は問題用紙に印刷されています。

リーディング

＊リスニングと同様、試験中にメモを取ることは禁止されています。

■ PART 5 短文穴埋め問題（30問）

1つの英文に1つの空所があり、選択肢から最も適切なものを選びます。

■ PART 6 長文穴埋め問題（16問）

1つの長文につき、4つの空所があります。4つのうち3つは語句を入れる問題ですが、1つだけ文章を入れる問題があります。

■ PART 7 読解問題（54問）

1つの文章、あるいは複数の文章（ダブル・パッセージ、トリプル・パッセージ）を読み、メールや手紙、記事、広告などさまざまなタイプの英文に関する設問を解きます。文章の種類に応じて設問の数も2問から5問まで分かれています。

CONTENTS

*PART 5は毎章学習します。

基礎編

応用編

Unit 1　品　詞

このユニットの文法事項では、品詞を学習します。また、リスニングセクションでは写真に関する基本的な問題を解くことで頻出表現を確認します。リーディングセクションについては、PART 6形式の空欄補充問題を通して、頻出語句や、このユニットで学習した文法事項などを確認します。

Word Check

次の各語句の意味を下から選びましょう。

1. useful　（　　　　）　**2.** increase　（　　　　）　**3.** inspect　（　　　　）

4. attend　（　　　　）　**5.** survey　（　　　　）　**6.** previous　（　　　　）

7. expensive（　　　　）　**8.** accessible（　　　　）　**9.** refund　（　　　　）

10. distributor（　　　　）

（A）到達できる　（B）返金　　（C）点検する　　（D）出席する　　（E）以前の
（F）有益な　　（G）販売店　　（H）調査　　　（I）高価な　　　（J）増える

Grammar Section

■品詞とは？

（1）名　詞：人や物、概念などの名称を表すもの：desk / Tom / Japan ...

（2）動　詞：行為、動作、状態などを表すもの：have / know / see ...

（3）形容詞：①名詞を修飾する：good / long / big ...
　　　　　　②be動詞などの補語になる

（4）副　詞：名詞以外のものを修飾するもの：very / much / suddenly ...

1 名詞に関する注意事項

（1）名詞は主語、目的語、補語として働くことができる。

（2）可算名詞と不可算名詞の違い

　　可算名詞（数えられる名詞）：普通名詞／集合名詞

　　不可算名詞（数えられない名詞）：物質名詞／抽象名詞／固有名詞／集合名詞の一部

　　＊注意すべき不可算名詞

　　 advice, baggage, luggage, equipment, furniture, information ...

| 例 題 | （　　　）内に入る最も適当なものを選んでみましょう。

1. His （　　　　）very useful for us.

　　（A）advice was　　　　　　（B）advices were

2. The book gives us （　　　　）about England.

　　（A）many informations　　　（B）much information

② 動詞に関する注意事項

(1) 主語と動詞の一致

① 英語では、主語の人称と数に応じて動詞の形が変化する。

I take a walk every morning.（一人称）

Our manager takes a walk every morning.（三人称・単数・現在）

② また、次のような表現では、主語と動詞の一致に注意。

The number of students who want to study abroad has been increasing.（単数扱い）

A number of students have recently been studying abroad.（複数扱い）

Not only the managers but also the president was absent from the meeting.

*not only A but also Bが主語の場合、動詞はBに合わせる。

③ 形容詞に関する注意事項

(1) 名詞を修飾する際の語順

冠詞＋形容詞（ -ful, -ive, -al, -ous, -icなどの語尾が多い）＋名詞

Mr. Davis gave a wonderful speech at the party.

(2) 補語としての働き

be動詞＋形容詞／look, seem, sound, feel ... ＋形容詞

The woman looked nice in that red dress.

④ 副詞に関する注意事項

(1) 副詞（-lyで終わるものが多い）は、名詞以外を修飾する修飾語句として働く。

Bill opened the letter *carefully.*（文末）

Fortunately, Michael succeeded in his first audition and got a part with lines.（文頭）

Mr. Wilde is *always* complaining about our company's policy.（動詞の近く）

例題 （　　）内に入る最も適当なものを選んでみましょう。

3. Our research team inspected the（　　　　）building.

(A) historic

(B) historically

4. He（　　　　）made the same mistakes.

(A) repeated

(B) repeatedly

5. （　　　　）, our shop closes at 9:00 P.M.

(A) Normal

(B) Normally

6. Either you or the manager（　　　　）to attend the meeting.

(A) have

(B) has

5 〈応用〉比較表現

形容詞と副詞は、「比較」の表現においては、形が変化したり、他の語句とセットで使われたりします。

(1) 3種類の比較表現と「級」

①「…と同じくらい〜である」 : 比較の結果が同等である場合

②「…より〜である」 : 一方が他方より程度が高い場合

③「…の中で最も〜である」 : 最も程度が高いものを表す場合

それぞれの比較表現に3種類の級 ── 原級、比較級、最上級 ── が対応します。

①He is as *tall* as Jim. : as + **原級** + as + 主格

②He is *taller* than Jim. : **比較級** + than + 主格 (SV)

③He is the *tallest* in this class. : the + **最上級** + in (of) 〜

(2) 比較級と最上級の変化のパターン

①規則変化1　原級の語尾に- (e) r、- (e) stをつけて、1語で比較級と最上級を表す

②規則変化2　原級の前にmore、mostを置いて、2語で比較級と最上級を表す

　　　　　　→規則変化2のルールが適用されるのは、原則として、母音が3つ以上含まれる語である。

③不規則変化　完全に形が変わるもの

　　　　　　good (well) , bad (badly) , many, much, little

(3) 程度や差異などを表す語句は比較級の前に置く

Jack is a little (much / three years ...) younger than I.

例 題 (　　　) 内に入る最も適当なものを選んでみましょう。

7. The newly released air conditioner has not sold as (　　　) as we expected.

(A) well　　　　　　　　(B) better

8. The population of this city is three times (　　　) than that of our city.

(A) largest　　　　　　(B) larger

次の問題を解きましょう。

1. In the most recent research, we focused on customers' (　　　) for domestic products rather than imported ones.

   (A) prefer　　　　　　　　(C) preferably
   (B) preferable　　　　　　(D) preference

2. According to a survey, online spending has increased globally but spending within stores has remained (　　　) stable.

   (A) relative　　　　　　　(C) relation
   (B) relatives　　　　　　 (D) relatively

3. Mr. Anderson's staff was always (　　　) to him.

   (A) loyal　　　　　　　　(C) loyalty
   (B) loyally　　　　　　　(D) loyalness

4. TS Electronics is one of (　　　) companies in this country.

   (A) large as　　　　　　　(C) larger than
   (B) the largest　　　　　 (D) most large

5. Tickets for the concert were (　　　) expensive than we expected.

   (A) a few　　　　(B) fewer　　　　(C) less　　　　(D) much

6. There are (　　　) three hundred workers at this branch.

   (A) approximate　　　　　(C) approximating
   (B) approximates　　　　 (D) approximately

7. Our new cellphone is (　　　) lighter than the previous one.

   (A) very　　　　(B) much　　　　(C) more　　　　(D) better

8. About 40% of our customers usually (　　　) the questionnaires.

   (A) answer　　　　　　　(C) is answered
   (B) answers　　　　　　 (D) has answered

9. Two thousand dollars for this watch (　　　) too expensive.

   (A) am　　　　(B) is　　　　(C) are　　　　(D) were

10. The department store is (　　　) accessible by car or subway.

    (A) easy　　　　　　　　(C) easiness
    (B) easily　　　　　　　(D) easier

このユニットのリスニングでは、PART 1の写真問題について基本的な問題を解いてみましょう。PART 1の基本問題としては、人物が何をしているかを問う問題が出題されます。写真に写っているのが1人の場合もあれば、複数の人たちが何をしているかが問われるときもありますので、注意しましょう。

例 題　音声を聞いて、(A)～(D) のなかでどれが正しいか選んでみましょう。　🔊 Audio① 02-05
　　　また、各文章の空欄には聞こえた語句を書いてみましょう。

1. Ⓐ Ⓑ Ⓒ Ⓓ

(A) He is ＿＿＿＿＿＿ on a platform.
(B) He is ＿＿＿＿＿＿ a newspaper.
(C) He is ＿＿＿＿＿＿ with a police officer.
(D) He is ＿＿＿＿＿＿ on the lawn.

2. Ⓐ Ⓑ Ⓒ Ⓓ

(A) They are ＿＿＿＿＿＿ on a bus.
(B) They are ＿＿＿＿＿＿ concert tickets.
(C) They are ＿＿＿＿＿ at the intersection.
(D) A man is ＿＿＿＿＿＿ at a map.

3. Ⓐ Ⓑ Ⓒ Ⓓ

(A) A boy is ＿＿＿＿＿＿ with a ball.
(B) Some people are ＿＿＿＿＿ on a bench.
(C) A boy is ＿＿＿＿＿＿ a bird.
(D) A boy is ＿＿＿＿＿ a pair of binoculars.

練習問題 音声を聞いて、(A)〜(D)のなかでどれが正しいか選びましょう。　📶 **Audio①** 06-09

1. Ⓐ Ⓑ Ⓒ Ⓓ

2. Ⓐ Ⓑ Ⓒ Ⓓ

3. Ⓐ Ⓑ Ⓒ Ⓓ

このユニットのリーディングでは、PART 6の問題について基本問題を解いてみましょう。

PART 6の基本問題としては、基本的な英語構文や文法事項を問う問題などがあげられます。このユニットで学習した品詞に関して、もう一度確認しましょう。

例 題 次の英文を読み、各空所に入る最も適切なものを選んでみましょう。

Questions 1-4 refer to the following notice.

Product Recall

It has come to the attention of us here at Funko that some customers are -- **1.** -- problems with the FunTrike tricycle that has been on sale at our stores since last year. Customers have been reporting that the handlebars of the tricycle can come -- **2.** --. As we consider your children's safety to be of utmost -- **3.** --, we would like to ask those customers who have bought the tricycle to return it to any of our Funko stores for a full refund. -- **4.** --.

---

1. (A) enjoying
   (B) experiencing
   (C) affecting

2. (A) loose
   (B) loosely
   (C) loosen

3. (A) important
   (B) importance
   (C) importantly

4. (A) The FunTrike is not so expensive.
   (B) We apologize for any inconvenience.
   (C) You can place your order online.

Questions 1-4 refer to the following advertisement.

GAME EAGLE
A new game distribution service

Do you like to play new video games as -- **1.** -- as they are available? Do you find other online stores -- **2.** -- expensive? Come and try Game Eagle, a new digital distributor of all your favorite games. We promise to offer you the newest games at the -- **3.** -- prices guaranteed! Sign up with Game Eagle and we will send you monthly up-to-date information of all the best new games available for your devices. As an introductory offer, if you buy a game from us before this December 25, we will send you a link to download a second game of your choice for free! -- **4.** -- .

1. (A) fast
    (B) soon
    (C) easy
    (D) cheap

2. (A) too
    (B) to
    (C) as
    (D) for

3. (A) smallest
    (B) lowest
    (C) biggest
    (D) easiest

4. (A) You will not be able to play it.
    (B) Don't miss this great opportunity!
    (C) We will be unable to help you any further.
    (D) We will be opening a new store near you soon!

Unit 2 — 時 制

 PART 2  **PART 7**

このユニットの文法事項では、時制を学習します。また、リスニングセクションではPART 2に関する基本的な問題を解くことで頻出する問題パターンを確認します。リーディングセクションについては、PART 7形式の読解問題（シングル・パッセージ）を通して、頻出する問題パターンや頻出語句を確認します。

Word Check

次の各語句の意味を下から選びましょう。

1. secretary （　　） 　 2. currently （　　） 　 3. deal （　　）

4. foundation （　　） 　 5. destination （　　） 　 6. applicant （　　）

7. leading （　　） 　 8. itinerary （　　） 　 9. inhabitant （　　）

10. sales representative （　　）

(A) 取引	(B) 旅行日程	(C) 住民	(D) 応募者	(E) 秘書
(F) 現在	(G) 販売員	(H) 主要な	(I) 設立	(J) 目的地

Grammar Section

■ 時制

1 時制の種類

（1）**現在**：現在の行動、事実、習慣など

　be動詞：am / are / is

　一般動詞：三単現のs（es）に注意

　*TOEIC® L&Rでは、usually、at present、またはcurrentlyなどの語句が一緒に用いられることがある。

　　Our secretary <u>usually</u> *goes* to the nearest fitness club after work.

　　Unfortunately, the item is <u>currently</u> out of order.

（2）**過去**：過去の行動、事実、習慣など

　be動詞：was / were

　一般動詞：規則変化（-ed, -d）／不規則変化

　*TOEIC® L&Rでは、文の中にlast、ago、in ＋ 過去の年代などが用いられることが多い。

　　The sales representative sent an e-mail to one of our customers <u>last Monday</u>.

（3）**未来**：未来の予定、推量、話者の意思など

　will ＋ 動詞の原形

　be going to ＋ 動詞の原形

　現在形（公的な予定）と現在進行形（個人的な予定）も未来を表現できる。

＊TOEIC® L&Rでは、nextや、in（時の経過を表す）などと一緒に用いられることがある。

The meeting *will* finish in another 30 minutes.

＊時（When「…の時」）や条件（If「もし…なら」）の副詞節では、未来の内容でも現在形を用いる。

When you *finish* the job, we will start the sales meeting.

(4) 進行形：進行中の行為、反復的動作、近未来（現在進行形）など

現在進行形：am / are / is ＋~ing（「…している」）

過去進行形：was / were ＋~ing（「…していた」）

未来進行形：will be ＋ ~ing（「…しているだろう、する予定」）

We *will be opening* another restaurant in Tokyo next month.

(5) 完了形：完了、継続、経験、結果

（A）現在完了形：have（has）＋ 過去分詞

（B）過去完了形：had ＋ 過去分詞

＊TOEIC® L&Rでは、for ＋ 期間、since ＋ 過去の年代などと一緒に用いられることが多い。

Our company *has contributed* much to the local community since its foundation in 1960.

Mr. Loomba *had worked* at an advertising company for three years before he joined our food company.

＊また、「継続」の意味を表わす場合のみ、完了進行形（have been ＋ ~ing）が用いられる場合がある。

Mr. Kawano *has been studying* psychology at college for two years.

（C）未来完了形：will have ＋ 過去分詞

＊TOEIC® L&Rでは、for ＋ 期間、加えて、by this time next year などと一緒に用いられることが多い。

The product *will have been* on the market for 10 years by the end of next month.

例題 （　　）内に入る最も適当なものを選んでみましょう。

1. **Our company has recently（** launching / launched **）its latest laptop.**

2. **Mr. Ottoman usually（** goes / has gone **）out for lunch with his colleagues.**

3. **All employees（** attend / attended **）the seminar yesterday afternoon.**

4. **The new regulation（** will be / was **）put into effect from the beginning of next month.**

次の問題を解きましょう。

1. My coworkers have (　　　　　) any items online.

   (A) orders　　　　　　　　　(C) never ordered
   (B) ordering　　　　　　　　(D) just order

2. Ms. Siegel (　　　　　) on a business trip to Shanghai next week.

   (A) went　　　　　　　　　　(C) has been
   (B) is going　　　　　　　　(D) have gone

3. As soon as it (　　　　) raining, we are going to leave for the destination.

   (A) stop　　　　(B) stops　　　　(C) will stop　　　　(D) will be stopped

4. Steve (　　　　) you some data regarding the online sales in two days.

   (A) send　　　　(B) will send　　　　(C) sending　　　　(D) is sent

5. Mr. Stone (　　　　) for this company for twenty years until he retired last year.

   (A) has worked　　　　　　(C) had worked
   (B) was worked　　　　　　(D) is working

6. Mr. Norman (　　　　) for this company for twenty years by this time next year.

   (A) has worked　　　　　　(C) will have worked
   (B) is working　　　　　　(D) had worked

7. Mr. Stevens (　　　　) the workshop on marketing at present, so he is not in the office.

   (A) is attended　　　　　　(C) was attending
   (B) is attending　　　　　　(D) attended

8. Some applicants (　　　　) us regarding a job interview this morning.

   (A) were called　　(B) calls　　　　(C) called　　　　(D) was calling

9. Tasty Noodle, one of the leading food companies in Japan, (　　　　) in 1977.

   (A) found　　　　　　　　　(C) founded
   (B) is founded　　　　　　(D) was founded

10. Our president said that he (　　　　) out of office next Friday to inspect another branch office.

    (A) has been　　　　　　　(C) would be
    (B) had been　　　　　　　(D) were

このユニットのリスニングでは、PART 2の問いかけ問題について、基本的な問題を解いてみましょう。
PART 2の基本問題としては、WhenやWhere、またはHowやWhyなどで始まる問いかけの問題が
出題されます。どの疑問詞で始まっているのかを聞き逃さないように、最初から注意して聞きましょう。

| 例 題 | 音声を聞いて、（A）～（C）のなかでどれが正しいか選んでみましょう。　🔊 Audio① 10-13
また、下にあるスクリプトの空欄には聞こえた語句を書いてみましょう。

1. Ⓐ Ⓑ Ⓒ

2. Ⓐ Ⓑ Ⓒ

3. Ⓐ Ⓑ Ⓒ

《スクリプト》　🔊 Audio① 11-13

1. _____ changed our itinerary?

　（A）Michael did.

　（B）I visited a travel agency.

　（C）I haven't gotten a ticket yet.

2. _____ are you supposed to give a presentation?

　（A）His presentation was really good.

　（B）Next Tuesday.

　（C）I have some meetings today.

3. _____ _____ file cabinets are there in your new office?

　（A）Some people are working in the office.

　（B）We cannot enter the cabin.

　（C）I'm not sure.

| 練習問題 | 音声を聞いて、（A）～（C）のなかでどれが正しいか選びましょう。　🔊 Audio① 14-24

1. Ⓐ Ⓑ Ⓒ　　　**6.** Ⓐ Ⓑ Ⓒ

2. Ⓐ Ⓑ Ⓒ　　　**7.** Ⓐ Ⓑ Ⓒ

3. Ⓐ Ⓑ Ⓒ　　　**8.** Ⓐ Ⓑ Ⓒ

4. Ⓐ Ⓑ Ⓒ　　　**9.** Ⓐ Ⓑ Ⓒ

5. Ⓐ Ⓑ Ⓒ　　**10.** Ⓐ Ⓑ Ⓒ

Reading Section **PART 7** 基本問題 広告やイベントのお知らせに関する問題

このユニットのリーディングでは、PART 7の問題について基本問題を解いてみましょう。
PART 7の基本問題としては、広告やイベントのお知らせなどに関する問題があります。比較的素直な問題が多いので、情報を正しく読み取りましょう。

| 例 題 | 次の文章を読んで、問いに答えてみましょう。

Questions 1-2 refer to the following information.

Annual Evening Concert for City Residents by Muse Quartet

Date : August 8
Time : 6:00 P.M. – 8:00 P.M.
Place : Civic Center (1F Music Hall)
Price : Free for city residents*
　　　$10 for others

*Please show some identification proving city residence at the entrance of the hall.

1.　Where can this information probably be found?

　　(A)　In a sports magazine
　　(B)　In a local newspaper
　　(C)　In an academic journal

2.　How much do people living in other cities have to pay for the concert?

　　(A)　$8
　　(B)　$10
　　(C)　Nothing

練習問題　次の文章を読んで、問いに答えましょう。

Questions 1-2 refer to the following advertisement.

Winter Sale at GSU!

We at GSU! will be offering 10-20% discounts on our items listed below from January 17 through 31.

10% OFF
Women's Coats
Sweaters for Men and Women
Men's Business Suits

20% OFF
Footwear for Men and Women

Come and take advantage of this special deal!

1. When will the sale begin?

　(A) January 10
　(B) January 17
　(C) January 20
　(D) January 31

2. Which items will be discounted by 20%?

　(A) Women's coats
　(B) Men's shoes
　(C) Men's suits
　(D) Women's sweaters

このユニットの文法事項では、受動態を学習します。また、リスニングセクションではPART 3に関する基本的な問題を解くことで頻出する問題パターンを確認します。リーディングセクションについては、PART 6形式の空欄補充問題を通して、頻出語句や、このユニットで学習した文法事項などを確認します。

Word Check

次の各語句の意味を下から選びましょう。

1. nominate （　　） **2.** reservation （　　） **3.** relocate （　　）

4. renovation （　　） **5.** defective （　　） **6.** participate in （　　）

7. order （　　） **8.** anniversary （　　） **9.** celebration （　　）

10. keynote speech （　　）

(A) 記念　　(B) 注文する　　(C) 欠陥のある　　(D) …に参加する　　(E) 選ぶ

(F) 予約　　(G) 改装　　(H) お祝い　　(I) 移動させる　　(J) 基調講演

Grammar Section

■ 受動態

1 能動態と受動態

下の①のように、「〜する（した）」のタイプの動詞を用いる文を能動態の文と呼ぶ。それに対して、②の英文を受動態の文と呼ぶ。受動態の文では動詞の形は、「be動詞 + 過去分詞」となり、原則として、「…が（は）〜される（された）」と訳す。

① Tom *cleans* this room every day.

② This room *is cleaned* by Tom every day.

2 by以外の前置詞を用いる場合

受動態ではby以外の前置詞を用いることがある。

- 〜に興味がある　be interested in 〜
- 〜に驚く　be surprised at 〜
- 〜に満足する　be satisfied with 〜
- 〜で覆われている　be covered with 〜
- 〜に知られている　be known to 〜
- 〜から作られている（材料）　be made of 〜
- 〜から作られている（原料）　be made from 〜

3 完了形の受動態と進行形の受動態

完了形の受動態は、have（has）+ been + 過去分詞の形になる。

Mr. Jennings *has been nominated* as chairperson.

また、進行形の受動態では、be動詞 + being + 過去分詞（「…されているところだ」）の形となる。

Flowers *are being watered* by a woman.

1. Robbie （　　　　） his friends to his new house.

   (A) invited　　　　　　　　(B) was invited

2. This desk is made （　　　　） wood.

   (A) of　　　　　　　　(B) by

3. Reservations for the rooms should （　　　　） at least two weeks in advance.

   (A) make　　　　　　　　(B) be made

練習問題

次の問題を解きましょう。

1. Our branch office （　　　　） from Manchester to Brighton last month.

   (A) relocates　　　　　(C) will relocate

   (B) is relocated　　　　(D) was relocated

2. Renovations to our company's cafeteria are currently （　　　　） made, so we have to go out for lunch.

   (A) be　　　　(B) been　　　　(C) being　　　　(D) to being

3. The next workshop （　　　　） to be held on Tuesday.

   (A) schedule　　　　　(C) is scheduled

   (B) scheduled　　　　(D) has scheduled

4. Our latest digital camera, the BXW-30, has to （　　　　） because of some defective parts.

   (A) recall　　　　(B) recalls　　　　(C) be recalling　　　　(D) be recalled

5. The largest room on this floor （　　　　） for the sales meeting this afternoon.

   (A) reserves　　　　　(C) is reserving

   (B) has reserved　　　(D) has been reserved

6. All new employees are （　　　　） to participate in the seminar scheduled for this afternoon.

   (A) entitle　　　　(B) entitles　　　　(C) entitled　　　　(D) entitling

7. Documents for the upcoming board meeting have to （　　　　） at least two days in advance.

   (A) prepare　　　　(B) prepared　　　　(C) be prepared　　　　(D) have prepared

8. Ms. Evans is known （　　　） everyone in this town for her spontaneous charity activities.

(A) with　　　　　(B) to　　　　　(C) by　　　　　(D) from

9. C. S. Daniel, an apparel brand popular among teenagers, （　　　） a new clothing line this summer.

(A) is launched　　　　　(C) will launch
(B) have launched　　　　(D) will be launched

10. On behalf of the company, our manager is （　　　） to give a keynote speech at the conference.

(A) suppose　　　(B) supposed　　　(C) supposes　　　(D) supposition

Listening Section　PART 3　会話の場所やトピック、電話の理由を問う問題

このユニットのリスニングでは、PART 3の会話文について基本的な問題を解いてみましょう。PART 3の基本問題としては、会話の場所やトピック、電話の理由などを問う問題が出題されます。とくに最初の話者が、会話の場所やトピック、電話の理由を示すヒントを言う可能性が高いので会話のはじまりから注意して聞きましょう。

例題　音声を聞いて、(A)〜(D)のなかでどれが正しいか選んでみましょう。　🔊 Audio① 25-29
また、下にあるスクリプトの空欄には聞こえた語句を書いてみましょう。

Questions 1-3 refer to the following conversation.

1. Where is the conversation most likely taking place?

(A) In the garden　　　　(C) At the garden center
(B) In the house　　　　(D) In the car

2. Why has the woman drawn a picture?

(A) She won't have time to draw it on the weekend.
(B) She wants to change how her garden looks.
(C) Leon asked her to draw something.
(D) She is feeling tired.

3. What are the speakers going to do on the weekend?

(A) Draw some more pictures of the garden
(B) Maintain the lawn in the garden
(C) Make a new homepage
(D) Do some gardening

W: Come in, Leon. Go through to the kitchen. I've made you a cup of tea.

M: Thanks. Wow. That's a colorful picture you've drawn. What is it?

W: It's my ¹_____ . I mean it's a plan of what I want to do with it. At the moment it's a mess and I want to ²_____ it.

M: Sounds like a great idea. What's the green part that you've drawn there?

W: Well, that's the lawn. Ha-ha. I'm not very good at drawing.

M: Lawns can grow ³_____ and they can be tricky to maintain. If you have flowers, I think it's better to have a good ⁴_____ . You should choose some that bloom all through the year.

W: Perfect! Hey, thanks for the ⁵_____ .

M: No problem. Actually, I have some time this weekend. Why don't we both go to the garden center, ⁶_____ what we need and get ⁷_____ on your garden?

W: Thanks. That would be great!

練習問題 | 音声を聞いて、（A）～（D）のなかでどれが正しいか選びましょう。　🔊 Audio① 30-34

Questions 1-3 refer to the following conversation.

1. Why does the woman call the man?

(A) To introduce him to White Smiles Dental Clinic

(B) To check an appointment

(C) To cancel his appointment

(D) To place an order

2. Why can't the man go at his original appointment time?

(A) Dr. Patel's meeting will not be finished by then.

(B) He has to make something at his work.

(C) His appointment has been canceled.

(D) He has to attend a meeting at his work.

3. What time is the man's new appointment?

(A) Thursday from 2 P.M.

(B) Friday at 4:30 P.M.

(C) Thursday at 4:30 P.M.

(D) Friday from 3:00 P.M.

このユニットのリーディングでは、PART 6の問題について基本問題を解いてみましょう。
PART 6の基本問題としては、基本的な英語構文や文法事項を問う問題などがあげられます。このユニットで学習した受動態に関して、もう一度確認しましょう。

例 題 次の英文を読み、各空所に入る最も適切なものを選んでみましょう。

Questions 1-4 refer to the following advertisement.

Mother's day is coming soon! **-- 1. --** send your mother some flowers to say "Thank You" from MeFlowers? MeFlowers has been delighting people on their birthdays, anniversaries and for all kinds of celebrations for 50 years. You can choose from our huge range of bouquets and baskets full of the flowers of your choice. If you prefer to let us choose for you, our **-- 2. --** staff can make a beautiful arrangement for your loved one. We also offer message cards and even chocolates to go with your gift. Are you ordering at the last minute? Don't worry! **-- 3. --** . Payment **-- 4. --** by credit card only. Start now by choosing your flowers from the selection below.

1. (A) Why not
   (B) Please
   (C) Where do you

2. (A) tired
   (B) experienced
   (C) expired

3. (A) Our flowers will take one week to arrive.
   (B) We guarantee next day delivery.
   (C) We cannot promise delivery on time.

4. (A) makes
   (B) is making
   (C) is made

Questions 1-4 refer to the following letter.

Dear Uncle Brian,

I am sorry that I haven't written to you for so long. Actually, I haven't written a letter to -- **1.** -- for a long time. These days, I am much more used to writing short e-mails to my friends and the rest of our family, or chatting to them online. -- **2.** --, you are the only person that I know that hasn't got an e-mail address! Anyway, I just wanted to wish you a happy birthday. Shunsuke and I have bought you a surprise present. It should -- **3.** -- tomorrow. -- **4.** --. I'll tell you. It is a new PC. We actually paid for you to get connected to the Internet too! As soon as you can, please write me an e-mail!
Speak to you soon.

Love,
Mai

1. (A) somebody
   (B) anybody
   (C) everyone
   (D) no-one

2. (A) In fact
   (B) Although
   (C) Take it easy
   (D) He said

3. (A) deliver
   (B) have delivered
   (C) be delivered
   (D) delivery

4. (A) Can you guess what it is?
   (B) Are you ready to go out?
   (C) Can you tell me your address?
   (D) What is your e-mail address?

不定詞・動名詞

このユニットの文法事項では、不定詞と動名詞を学習します。また、リスニングセクションではPART 4に関する基本的な問題を解くことで頻出する問題パターンを確認します。リーディングセクションについては、PART 7形式の読解問題 (シングル・パッセージ、ダブル・パッセージ) を通して、頻出する問題パターンや頻出語句を確認します。

Word Check

次の各語句の意味を下から選びましょう。

1. plenty of （　　） **2.** client （　　） **3.** encourage （　　）

4. regarding （　　） **5.** budget （　　） **6.** in charge of （　　）

7. brochure （　　） **8.** available （　　） **9.** attach （　　）

10. do not hesitate to （　　）

(A) …に関して　(B) 利用できる　　(C) たくさんの　(D) 顧客　　　　(E) 予算
(F) 促す　　　(G) 遠慮なく…する　(H) パンフレット　(I) …を担当して　(J) 添付する

Grammar Section

■不定詞

1 不定詞の基本形

不定詞は「to + 動詞の原形 (+α)」という形をとり、toの後ろの動詞は、時制や主語の人称、数に関係なく、原形になる。

2 不定詞の3用法

(1) 名詞用法

名詞と同様に文の主語、目的語、補語になる。原則として「〜すること」と訳す。

Mary decided *to go* to France.

(2) 形容詞用法

直前の名詞を修飾する。原則として「〜するための…」または「〜すべき…」と訳す。

We still have plenty of work left *to finish* by this weekend.

(3) 副詞用法

名詞以外の要素 (動詞、形容詞など) を修飾する。副詞用法には「目的」「原因・理由」「結果」など複数の種類がある。

Our manager went to Singapore last week *to inspect* the factory.

❸ 形式主語

名詞用法の不定詞句が主語となる場合、それをitで置き換え、不定詞句を後ろ（多くは文末）に置くことがある。このときに用いられるitは形式主語（仮主語）と呼ばれる。

To win the tournament is our goal. = *It* is our goal *to win the tournament*.

■ 動名詞

❶ 動名詞の基本形

動名詞は「動詞の原形＋-ing（＋α）」という形をとり、その名前の通り、動詞としての働きに名詞としての働きが加えられたもの。

❷ 動名詞の用法

動名詞は、一般に、「〜すること」と訳し、文中で主語、目的語、補語として働く。動名詞を用いる際には、次のことに注意が必要。

（1）前置詞の目的語になる動名詞

前置詞の目的語になることができるのは動名詞のみである。

She is fond *of taking* pictures.

他にも、look forward to 〜ing、get (be) used to 〜ingなどが頻出表現。

（2）動名詞と不定詞

両者はともに名詞と同様に一般動詞の目的語になるが、その場合には使い分けのルールがある。原則として、不定詞は未来（これから行うこと）、動名詞は現在・過去（今行っていること／すでに行ったこと）を含意する。

（A）動名詞のみを目的語とする動詞：avoid / consider / finish / enjoy / keepなど

（B）不定詞のみを目的語とする動詞：hope / decide / plan / promise / agreeなど

（C）動名詞と不定詞の両方を目的語にできる動詞

（a）どちらを使っても意味が同じ動詞：like / love / begin / startなど

（b）意味が異なる動詞：remember / forget / regret / tryなど

Do you remember *seeing him before*?（以前彼に会ったこと）

Do you remember *to see him today*?（今日彼に会うこと）

| 例 題 | （　　　）内に入る最も適当なものを選んでみましょう。

1. Don't forget（　　　　）your client tomorrow.

（A）to call　　　　　　　　　（B）calling

2. Muriel decided（　　　　）for the position at another company.

（A）to apply　　　　　　　　（B）applying

3. Thank you for（　　　　）me a quick reply.

（A）to send　　　　　　　　（B）sending

4. I really enjoyed（　　　　）the rugby game last night.

（A）watch　　　　　　　　　（B）watching

次の問題を解きましょう。

1. We are encouraged to attend the workshop (　　　　) how to deal with difficult customers.

   (A) learn　　　　(B) learns　　　　(C) to learn　　　　(D) to learning

2. Lenard didn't have a chance (　　　　) golf during his vacation.

   (A) play　　　　(B) to play　　　　(C) to playing　　　　(D) playing

3. Please do not hesitate (　　　　) me if you need further information.

   (A) contact　　　　　　　　(C) to contact
   (B) contacting　　　　　　　(D) contacted

4. We need to finish (　　　　) the budget plan by the end of the week.

   (A) make　　　　　　　　(C) to make
   (B) making　　　　　　　(D) made

5. Ms. Coleman is in charge of (　　　　) the brochure featuring our new line of furniture.

   (A) edit　　　　　　　　(C) being edited
   (B) editing　　　　　　　(D) edited

6. (　　　　) the shipment status of your order, please visit our web site.

   (A) Check　　　　　　　　(C) Checked
   (B) To check　　　　　　　(D) To be checked

7. When you send your file, please be sure (　　　　) it is encoded.

   (A) confirm　　　　　　　(C) to confirm
   (B) confirming　　　　　　(D) confirmed

8. (　　　　) things online is quick and easy, as well as cheaper.

   (A) Buy　　　　　　　　(C) To buying
   (B) Buying　　　　　　　(D) To bought

9. We are looking forward (　　　　) with you in the near future.

   (A) work　　　　(B) working　　　　(C) to work　　　　(D) to working

10. We had discussed for hours but Mr. Nash avoided (　　　　) on a roadmap for the new project.

    (A) agree　　　　　　　　(C) agreeing
    (B) to agree　　　　　　　(D) to agreeing

このユニットのリスニングでは、PART 4の説明文問題について基本的な問題を解いてみましょう。PART 4の基本問題としては、トークやアナウンスの目的や理由などを問う問題が出題されます。音声の前半で目的や理由が言われる可能性が高いので最初から注意して聞きましょう。

| 例 題 | 音声を聞いて、(A)～(D)のなかでどれが正しいか選んでみましょう。　🔊 Audio① 35-39
また、下にあるスクリプトの空欄には聞こえた語句を書いてみましょう。

Questions 1-3 refer to the following meeting announcement.

1. What is the meeting about?

   (A) To ask people to take care of their work-related belongings
   (B) To tell people to hand things in to the lost and found office
   (C) To ensure that people do not travel by train so much
   (D) To avoid traveling to Tokyo alone

2. What is said about the briefcase?

   (A) It was left on a train.
   (B) It did not have any sensitive data in it.
   (C) It was found at the head office.
   (D) It was left at the workplace.

3. What is said about work computers?

   (A) Many people have important data on them.
   (B) They should not be taken from the office.
   (C) People should not take them on the train.
   (D) They should be handed in to the lost and found office.

《スクリプト》　🔊 Audio① 36

Thanks for ¹_____ to this emergency meeting, everyone. I have just heard from our head office that one of our members of staff ²_____ his briefcase, which had his PC inside, on the ³_____ while on his way to Tokyo yesterday. Luckily, someone handed the briefcase, including the PC, into the ⁴_____ _____ _____ office at Tokyo Station. As you all know, many of us have sensitive ⁵_____ on our work computers, including company e-mails and passwords. Please be sure to take ⁶_____ of your work-related ⁷_____ whenever you take them from the ⁸_____ and make sure everything is password-protected.

練習問題 音声を聞いて、(A)〜(D)のなかでどれが正しいか選びましょう。　🔊 Audio① 40-44

Questions 1-3 refer to the following talk.

1. What is the purpose of this talk?

   (A) To show appreciation to employees

   (B) To give information about the company event

   (C) To report the weather forecast

   (D) To apologize for the delay in shipping

2. What is mentioned about Ms. Popat?

   (A) She was the most successful worker in East Japan.

   (B) Her advertising campaign was disappointing.

   (C) She will not receive regular year-end holidays.

   (D) She and her team made a good advertising campaign.

3. What benefit does the speaker say his staff will receive?

   (A) Extra money in next month's salary

   (B) A chance to appear in a TV commercial for the company

   (C) Extra holiday time

   (D) A free product

このユニットのリーディングでは、PART 7の問題について基本問題を解いてみましょう。
PART 7の基本問題としては、メールなどの目的や理由などを問う問題などがあげられます。その際には、同じ意味の語句の言いかえなどに注意しましょう。

例 題 次の文章を読んで、問いに答えてみましょう。

Questions 1-2 refer to the following e-mail.

To   : allstaff@marten.com
From   : Libby_Jinner@marten.com
Subject : health check-up 🖉

Our company's annual free health check-up will take place next week. There are two sessions available, one on Wednesday morning and another on Friday afternoon. Please complete the attached form to show when you will attend and e-mail it back to us soon. In addition to the regular physical examination, a nutritionist as well as a gym instructor will be there to answer any questions you have concerning your diet and help you to create realistic exercise plans. We believe that a healthy company needs healthy workers, so please try and attend one of the available sessions.

Libby Jinner,
General Manager

---

1. Why was this e-mail sent?

   (A) To encourage employees to eat a healthy diet

   (B) To answer some questions about employees' health

   (C) To ask employees to attend a health check-up

   (D) To make employees do regular exercise

2. What should workers do after reading this e-mail?

   (A) Send a reply regarding their health check date

   (B) Exercise to improve their health

   (C) Ask some questions to a nutritionist

   (D) Visit an exercise specialist in a gym downtown

Questions 1-4 refer to the following e-mails.

Subject : Complaint
Date   : January 20

Dear Sir,
I am writing to complain about the service that I received during a meal this afternoon at your restaurant, The Indian Palace. I made a reservation for four people to eat lunch there three days ago. However, when I arrived at the restaurant with my friends, we were told that the restaurant was full and that there was no record of my reservation. We had to wait for 30 minutes before we could sit down. After we had ordered the food, we had to wait for 30 more minutes before it arrived. Although it was delicious, we had to eat it quickly as we needed to return to work for the afternoon. I look forward to hearing from you.

Yours faithfully,
Matt Pope

Subject : Re: Complaint
Date   : January 21

Dear Mr. Pope,
Thank you very much for your e-mail. I am sorry to hear that you didn't enjoy your time at The Indian Palace yesterday. Firstly, with regard to your reservation, it seems that there was a problem with our website until yesterday and that is why your online reservation did not work. I am pleased to say that our website is now working properly. As for your complaint regarding the slow service, we have a new chef who is just learning how to use the modern tools in our kitchen. I am sure that he will be able to cook at a faster speed soon. I am very happy that you enjoyed the food. As an apology, I would like to offer you and your friends a free replacement meal. Please use the website again and make a reservation for a date convenient for you. In the discount code section on the reservation page, please use the code '23pope'.

Best regards,
Assad Singh, Owner, The Indian Palace

1. **What was the first problem that Mr. Pope and his friends had at the restaurant?**

   (A) The chef was not at the restaurant.
   (B) Their reservation had not been registered.
   (C) The food was not good.
   (D) They had to return to their office to fix a computer problem.

2. **Why did Mr. Pope and his friends have to wait for another 30 minutes after sitting down?**

   (A) The restaurant was very noisy.
   (B) There was a problem with a computer.
   (C) The chef wasn't used to using the kitchen tools.
   (D) The waiter forgot to take an order.

3. **What does Mr. Singh offer as an apology to Mr. Pope and his friends?**

   (A) Mr. Pope and his friends can visit the kitchens of the restaurant to see their food being made.
   (B) He will give Mr. Pope and his friends a full refund.
   (C) He will get another chef to work in his restaurant as soon as possible.
   (D) Mr. Pope and his friends can eat at the restaurant for free after making a reservation.

4. **In the second e-mail, the word "convenient" in paragraph 1, line 10, is closest in meaning to**

   (A) speedy
   (B) dominant
   (C) memorable
   (D) suitable

このユニットの文法事項では、分詞を学習します。また、リスニングセクションでは写真に関する基本的な問題を解くことで頻出表現を確認します。リーディングセクションについては、PART 6形式の空欄補充問題を通して、頻出語句や、このユニットで学習した文法事項などを確認します。

Word Check

次の各語句の意味を下から選びましょう。

1. construction site（　　）　　2. material 　　（　　）　　3. stock price 　（　　）

4. invest 　　（　　）　　5. light fixture （　　）　　6. spread 　　（　　）

7. rapidly 　　（　　）　　8. application （　　）　　9. negotiation （　　）

10. economic downturn 　　（　　）

(A) 急激に	(B) 投資する	(C) 不景気	(D) 応募	(E) 株価
(F) 建設現場	(G) 照明器具	(H) 交渉	(I) 材料・物質	(J) 広がる

Grammar Section

1 分詞の形容詞用法（1）　限定用法

（1）構文

分詞を形容詞として用い、名詞を修飾する際には、分詞を単独で使う場合と、分詞と他の語句とともに、つまり句の形で使う場合で、名詞との位置関係が異なる。

①分詞が単独で名詞を修飾するときは、その名詞の前に置かれ、「分詞＋名詞」の語順になる。

She looked at the sleeping baby.

②分詞が他の語句とともに句の形で名詞を修飾するときは、名詞の後に置かれ、「名詞＋分詞＋他の語句」となる。

She looked at the baby sleeping on the sofa.

（2）現在分詞／過去分詞の選択

①現在分詞は「〜している」、過去分詞は「〜される」という意味で使い分ける。

The man closing the gate over there is my uncle.

②ただし、自ら動くことが普通できないものについては、日本語で「〜している」と訳せる場合でも英語では過去分詞を使う。

He was standing by the closed gate.

例題 （　　）内に入る最も適当なものを選んでみましょう。

1. His team successfully repaired the (breaking / broken) projector.

2. The man (worn / wearing) a white jacket is our manager.

(3) 注意すべき表現

感情を表す動詞 (surprise、amaze、satisfyなど) は、その感情を引き起こさせるという意味を持っているため、現在分詞と過去分詞の選択に注意が必要となる。

There were a lot of people annoyed by the noise from the construction site.

The noise annoying a lot of people came from the construction site.

例題 （　　）内に入る最も適当なものを選んでみましょう。

3.　The stadium was filled with an (exciting / excited) audience.

4.　We found the (disappointing / disappointed) result of the game in the newspaper.

2 分詞の形容詞用法 (2)　叙述用法

(1) 第2文型の補語となる場合

一部の自動詞 (sit、stand、look、seem、remain、keep、come、walkなど) は分詞を補語とすることができる。

She kept talking to someone on the phone.

(2) 第5文型の補語となる場合

現在分詞の場合：OがCしている (していた)

I saw him cleaning the office this morning.

過去分詞の場合：OがCされる (された)、OがCされている (されていた)

You must keep the office cleaned.

3 分詞の副詞用法 (分詞構文)

(1) 構文

①主節と従属節の主語が同じ場合、接続詞と主語を省略し、動詞を分詞に変えることで、分詞構文の英文を作ることができる。その場合、「時」「理由」「条件」「譲歩」「付帯状況」のいずれかの意味となる。

When he lived in London, he often had fish and chips with his friends.

　→ Living in London, he often had fish and chips with his friends.

②従属節に受動態が用いられているときは、beingまで省略することもできる。

Because he was shocked by the first scene, he couldn't see the whole movie.

　→ Shocked by the first scene, he couldn't see the whole movie.

③従属節の時制が完了形、あるいは、主節より過去である場合は、分詞構文の動詞形をhaving+過去分詞にする。

Because she studied Japanese literature at college, she speaks good Japanese.

　→ Having studied Japanese literature at college, she speaks good Japanese.

④従属節が否定文の場合、分詞の前にnotを置く。

As I didn't know his mail address or phone number, I couldn't contact him.

　→Not knowing his mail address or phone number, I couldn't contact him.

⑤従属節と主節の主語が異なる場合、従属節の主語を残す。

If the weather is nice, we will camp by the lake for two days.

　→ The weather being nice, we will camp by the lake for two days.

| 例 題 | （　　）内に入る最も適当なものを選んでみましょう。|

5. （ Writing / Written) in simple English, the book is easy to understand.

6. （ Watching / Watched) the movie, I remembered my old friend.

(2) 慣用表現

分詞構文には数多くの慣用表現がある。これらは独立した表現として記憶しておくこと。

①〜から判断すると：judging from 〜

Judging from his accent, he must be from Ireland.

②〜を考慮すると：considering 〜

Considering his age, he needs to stay in the hospital for a while.

③もし〜ならば：providing 〜、provided 〜

We will buy these materials from you, providing all the conditions are met.

| 例 題 | （　　）内に入る最も適当なものを選んでみましょう。|

7. Japanese stock prices are now too high, (compared / comparing) to the recent trend.

8. You should invest in real estate, (considering / providing) the population growth in this city.

(3) 分詞構文の注意すべき形

分詞構文は、副詞節の接続詞と主語を省略して文を簡略化したものであるが、「時」「条件」など複数の意味の可能性があるため、接続詞を残し、どの意味で理解すべきかを明示することがある。そのとき、語順は「接続詞＋分詞」となる。

When she saw me, she waved her hand.

→ *Seeing* me, she waved her hand. （分詞構文）

→ *When seeing* me, she waved her hand. （接続詞を伴う分詞構文）

| 例 題 | 「接続詞＋分詞」の形の分詞構文を用いて、同内容の英文を書いてみましょう。|

9. While he was staying in Paris, he visited a lot of museums.

_____

10. Although he lived near the school, he was often late for school.

_____

次の問題を解きましょう。

1. Behind the (　　　) door several men were talking aloud.

   (A) closes　　　(B) to close　　　(C) be closing　　　(D) closed

2. There are some splendid light fixtures (　　　) from the ceiling in the room.

   (A) hang　　　(B) hangs　　　(C) hanging　　　(D) to hanging

3. Mr. Paterson has just read one of the most (　　　) essays he has ever seen in his 30-year teaching career.

   (A) amaze　　　(B) amazing　　　(C) amazed　　　(D) amazingly

4. What we saw was some (　　　) people who were complaining about how difficult it was to operate the new ATM.

   (A) irritate　　　(B) irritates　　　(C) irritated　　　(D) to irritate

5. This morning our boss walked in (　　　) gently with a big bag in his hand.

   (A) smiling　　　(B) smiled　　　(C) smile　　　(D) smiles

6. As soon as we sat back on the couch, we heard our secretary's name (　　　).

   (A) call　　　(B) to call　　　(C) calling　　　(D) called

7. The news of the bank's bankruptcy spread rapidly, (　　　) an economic downturn.

   (A) cause　　　　　　　(C) caused
   (B) causing　　　　　　(D) to be caused

8. (　　　) with the result of the negotiation, the CEOs of both companies sat in front of the press smiling.

   (A) Satisfy　　　　　　(C) Satisfied
   (B) Satisfying　　　　(D) Satisfaction

9. (　　　) as an engineer for 15 years, Jack knew how to solve such a problem.

   (A) Had been working　　　(C) Having been working
   (B) Worked　　　　　　　　(D) Have been working

10. The regular system maintenance, (　　　) the engineer's report, seemed successfully completed.

    (A) providing　　　　　(C) considered
    (B) judging from　　　(D) according

このユニットのリスニングでは、PART 1の写真問題について基本的な問題を解いてみましょう。PART 1の基本問題としては、物の状態や位置関係を問う問題が出題されます。写真中央に写っているもの以外のものの状態が問われるときもありますので、注意しましょう。

| 例 題 | 音声を聞いて、（A）〜（D）のなかでどれが正しいか選んでみましょう。　🔊 Audio① 45-48 |

また、各文章の空欄には聞こえた語句を書いてみましょう。

1. Ⓐ Ⓑ Ⓒ Ⓓ

(A) Books are ＿＿＿＿＿＿＿ up on the desk.

(B) Papers are ＿＿＿＿＿＿＿ on the floor.

(C) A man is ＿＿＿＿＿＿＿ a computer.

(D) The box is left ＿＿＿＿＿＿＿ .

2. Ⓐ Ⓑ Ⓒ Ⓓ

(A) The man is ＿＿＿＿＿＿＿ something into the trash can.

(B) Some people are ＿＿＿＿＿＿＿ TV.

(C) A woman is ＿＿＿＿＿＿＿ posters on the wall.

(D) There are some papers ＿＿＿＿＿＿＿ on the bulletin board.

3. Ⓐ Ⓑ Ⓒ Ⓓ

(A) People are ＿＿＿＿＿＿＿ chairs.

(B) Chairs are ＿＿＿＿＿＿＿ up on the stage.

(C) Some chairs are ＿＿＿＿＿＿＿ side by side.

(D) Some people are ＿＿＿＿＿＿＿ on the chairs.

練習問題 音声を聞いて、(A) 〜 (D) のなかでどれが正しいか選びましょう。　　🔊 Audio① 49-52

1. Ⓐ Ⓑ Ⓒ Ⓓ

2. Ⓐ Ⓑ Ⓒ Ⓓ

3. Ⓐ Ⓑ Ⓒ Ⓓ

このユニットのリーディングでは、PART 6の問題について基本問題を解いてみましょう。

PART 6の基本問題としては、基本的な英語構文や文法事項を問う問題などがあげられます。このユニットで学習した分詞に関して、もう一度確認しましょう。

> **例 題**　次の文章を読み、空欄に入る最も適切な語句を選んでみましょう。

Questions 1-4 refer to the following article.

> The annual children's TV show awards ceremony was held in Tokyo this weekend. Jane Sato, the presenter of the popular show *Bobby's Amazing Hat*, was -- **1.** -- a Lifetime Achievement Award. Ms. Sato has presented the show every Saturday morning for the -- **2.** -- 25 years. -- **3.** --. It features many ideas for making simple toys from everyday objects. Popular music acts often appear on the show, which makes it appealing to an older audience too. Ms. Sato said she was -- **4.** -- with the award. Speaking at the ceremony, she said: "I love presenting the show every week. It is an honor to receive this award today. I am looking forward to presenting *Bobby's Amazing Hat* for 25 more years!"

1. (A) gave

(B) given

(C) give

2. (A) past

(B) over

(C) total

3. (A) The show is very popular with young children.

(B) *Bobby's Amazing Hat* will not be shown after this year.

(C) The presenter of the show did not attend the ceremony.

4. (A) unhappy

(B) delighted

(C) disappointed

Questions 1-4 refer to the following introductions.

Welcome to our new passport website. When -- **1.** -- for your new passport, you will need to attach and send a digital photo with your online application. The photo must be -- **2.** -- with a white background. Make sure you are not wearing glasses in the photo and please do not smile. You can take the photo by yourself, -- **3.** --, for example, the camera on your cellphone. -- **4.** --. Now, please click on the 'Next' button below to begin your new passport application process.

1. (A) apply
  (B) applied
  (C) appliance
  (D) applying

2. (A) taken
  (B) took
  (C) taking
  (D) takes

3. (A) use
  (B) using
  (C) to using
  (D) used

4. (A) Thank you for your help.
  (B) Alternatively, you can ask someone to take it for you.
  (C) The new model is too expensive to buy.
  (D) Send him an e-mail when you are finished.

Unit 6 前置詞・接続詞

 PART 2  **PART 7**

このユニットの文法事項では、前置詞・接続詞を学習します。また、リスニングセクションではPART 2に関する頻出問題を解くことで問題パターンを確認します。リーディングセクションについては、PART 7形式の読解問題（シングル・パッセージ）を通して、頻出する問題パターンや頻出語句を確認していきます。

Word Check

次の各語句の意味を下から選びましょう。

1. permission （　　） 2. transportation （　　） 3. malfunction （　　）

4. investigation （　　） 5. warranty （　　） 6. valid （　　）

7. gradually （　　） 8. establish （　　） 9. revise （　　）

10. ongoing （　　）

（A）進行中の	（B）次第に	（C）設立する	（D）修正する	（E）有効な
（F）保証書	（G）許可	（H）交通機関	（I）不具合	（J）調査

Grammar Section

■ 前置詞・接続詞 ─────────────

1 前置詞

（1）注意すべき前置詞

● by

① 「…だけ」（程度）

Our sales increased by 10% last quarter.

② 「…までに」（期限）

The document needs to be submitted by next Friday.

③ 「…によって」（手段）

You can pay by check.

● until 「…まで」（継続）

The meeting continued until midnight.

● between 「…の間」（2つのもの）　*among 「…の間」は3つ以上のときに用いる。

The negotiation between the two companies ended in success.

● without 「…なしで」

No one can enter the room after 5:00 P.M. without permission.

● instead of 「…の代わりに」

Please use public transportation instead of your own cars.

● due to 「…のために」(= because of, owing to, thanks to)

Due to the bad weather, the picnic was canceled.

（2）前置詞の使い方

① 前置詞の後ろには名詞か代名詞、または動名詞が置かれる。前置詞のtoを含む熟語・慣用表現にはとくに注意が必要。

Mr. Hudson has gradually gotten accustomed to *dealing* with customers.

② 名詞と動名詞の両方が選択肢にあるときは、後ろに名詞が続かない限り、本来語である名詞を選択する。一方、後ろに名詞が続く場合、動名詞を選択する。

The cause of the elevator's malfunction is now under *investigation*.

| 例 題 | （　　）内に入る最も適当なものを選んでみましょう。

1. Many people came in (expecting / expectation) their questions to be answered.

2. This portable game machine is very popular (between / among) young people.

3. The warranty of the device is valid (by / for) three years.

4. Mr. Thomas eventually began to work (into / on) the assignment.

2 接続詞

（1）接続詞の役割

接続詞は語句と語句あるいは節と節をつなぐ働きをする。

Ms. Wilson appreciated the comments by Dr. Hector *and* colleagues on her paper.

You will be recommended to purchase a season pass *if* you would like to see the exhibition more than five times.

（2）注意すべき接続詞

● in case 「…の場合に備えて」

Remember his number in case there is any network trouble.

● once 「いったん…したら」

You should not open the envelope once you seal it.

● although 「…だけれども」

Although it rained heavily, the festival was very successful.

● since

①「…なので」

Please call us again later since the line is busy now.

②「…して以来」

We have lived in this city since we got married ten years ago.

● until 「…するまで」（継続）

Please keep your seatbelt fastened until the sign goes off.

(3) 接続詞に関する注意

① 時や条件を表す副詞節では、未来の事柄でも現在時制が使われる。

The strong yen trend will continue if Japan *sustains* steady growth.

② 前半と後半の主語が同じで、前半部分の動詞がbe動詞のとき、主語と動詞が省略されることがある。

While (he) (was) in London on business, Mr. Paterson lost his watch.

| 例 題 | (　　)内に入る最も適当なものを選んでみましょう。

5. Please feel free to call me anytime (because / if) you have any questions.

6. Customers often ask (that / if) we sell organic produce only.

7. (During / While) on duty, you must not use your smartphones.

8. Ms. Franklin was pleased with the news, (until / whereas) her boss seemed dissatisfied with it.

(4) 連語の接続詞

① so ~ that ... 「とても~なので…」

Digital content on the Internet is increasing so rapidly that no single search engine can index all of it.

② as soon as ~ 「~するとすぐに」

As soon as the merger was announced yesterday, the stock price of JPW Ltd. skyrocketed by over 30%.

③ either A or B 「AかBのどちらか」

Participants will be asked to attend either the symposium or the workshop.

④ neither A nor B 「AとBのどちらも~ない」

Our service targets the people who can afford neither a car nor a motorcycle.

⑤ not only A but (also) B 「AばかりでなくBも」

At Delight Evening, you can enjoy not only our authentic Polynesian cuisine but also a traditional and antique interior.

⑥ both A and B 「AとBの両方とも」

The abstracts will be available both at the meeting and on our website.

⑦ A as well as B 「Bと同じくAも」

Ms. McCarthy put a stress on the importance of systematic branding as well as strategical marketing.

(5) 接続副詞

PART 6で頻出する接続副詞には、therefore / consequently / however / nevertheless / moreover / furthermore / thus / meanwhile / insteadがある。

Jenifer visited Dr. Burton yesterday; however, he was out of office.

9. Antonio had been told to take enough rest; (although / nevertheless), he worked more than 50 hours overtime last month.

10. Christopher Macmillan always brings a camera with him (in case / in case of) he finds something interesting.

11. The successful candidate will be contacted either by e-mail (and / or) by phone.

練習問題

次の問題を解きましょう。

1. The meetings were held several times with the participation of a large number of residents of the city, (　　　　　) only a few supported the redevelopment project.

   (A) but　　　　　(B) if　　　　　(C) due to　　　　　(D) how

2. The fieldwork will continue tomorrow (　　　　) the weather changes dramatically.

   (A) if not　　　　(B) that　　　　(C) unless　　　　(D) during

3. All committee members should arrive here before the meeting (　　　　) at 10:30.

   (A) is going to start　　　　(C) will have started
   (B) will start　　　　　　　(D) starts

4. (　　　　) you know, our office has been relocated to Yokohama.

   (A) As　　　　(B) Because　　　　(C) Since　　　　(D) For

5. Nobody realized (　　　　) they would have to wait to see the movie star appear at the lobby.

   (A) because　　(B) although　　(C) for　　　(D) how long

6. Ms. Cheng was (　　　　) shocked by the condition of the room that she refused to stay any longer.

   (A) very　　　　(B) too　　　　(C) so　　　　(D) a little

7. A number of school buses were in service on that day (　　　　) the hurricane was raging.

   (A) during　　(B) while　　(C) nevertheless　　(D) because of

8. Many economists have warned (　　　　) the unemployment rate will increase gradually.

   (A) for　　　　(B) with　　　　(C) that　　　　(D) until

9. Illinois Green Ltd. has rapidly increased its market share since 2008 (   )
   it was established with only 5,000 dollars in capital.

   (A) despite   (B) in spite of   (C) however   (D) although

10. We are going to revise the ongoing project (   ) unpredictable changes.

   (A) in case of   (C) if
   (B) in the event that   (D) consequently

Listening Section PART 2 さまざまな疑問文や平叙文の問いかけ

このユニットのリスニングでは、PART 2の問いかけ問題について、頻出するさまざまなパターンの問題を解いてみましょう。付加疑問文や平叙文などもよく出題されるので、どのタイプなのかを聞き逃さないように注意して聞きましょう。

例題 音声を聞いて、(A)～(C)のなかでどれが正しいか選んでみましょう。　　　🔊 Audio① 53-56
     また、下にあるスクリプトの空欄には聞こえた語句を書いてみましょう。

1. Ⓐ Ⓑ Ⓒ   2. Ⓐ Ⓑ Ⓒ   3. Ⓐ Ⓑ Ⓒ

《スクリプト》 🔊 Audio① 54-56

1. _____ you think we should make a _____ with him?

   (A) It's up to you.
   (B) This is the first movie dealing with the incident.
   (C) He should do that.

2. Mr. Ferguson will _____ tomorrow, _____ he?

   (A) He wanted to live here.
   (B) Yes. We will be waiting at the airport.
   (C) Not at all.

3. I _____ _____ they called me back to the head office so soon.

   (A) They will call you at 10:30.
   (B) Because of your language proficiency, of course.
   (C) They told me to carry your bag.

練習問題 音声を聞いて、(A)～(C)のなかでどれが正しいか選びましょう。　　🔊 Audio① 57-67

1. Ⓐ Ⓑ Ⓒ   6. Ⓐ Ⓑ Ⓒ
2. Ⓐ Ⓑ Ⓒ   7. Ⓐ Ⓑ Ⓒ
3. Ⓐ Ⓑ Ⓒ   8. Ⓐ Ⓑ Ⓒ
4. Ⓐ Ⓑ Ⓒ   9. Ⓐ Ⓑ Ⓒ
5. Ⓐ Ⓑ Ⓒ   10. Ⓐ Ⓑ Ⓒ

このユニットのリーディングでは、PART 7の問題についてさまざまなパターンの問題を解いてみましょう。とくに、推測問題ははっきり書いていないことが多いので注意が必要です。また、文章挿入などに関する問題は、前後の内容から判断しましょう。

例題　次の文章を読んで、問いに答えてみましょう。

Questions 1-3 refer to the following e-mail.

Dear Ms. Wagner,

Thank you for your offer to write an article for the April issue of our magazine, *Enjoy Your Life*. — [1] — . The topic of the article is entirely up to you so long as it is one that will be exciting for our readers. — [2] — . However, there are three points we ask you to keep in mind. Firstly, as you know, most of our readers are women in their early twenties. Secondly, when you wrote on the newest trend of women's fashion items in our magazine last time, the feedback from readers was very favorable. — [3] — . Thirdly, please be aware that the deadline is the end of this month. Please send your draft directly to me as an attachment to your e-mail. Thanks in advance.

Susan Burton
Sunny Publishing

1.　What most likely is the relationship between Ms. Wagner and Ms. Burton?

　　(A)　A customer and a sales representative

　　(B)　A writer and an editor

　　(C)　A college student and a teacher

2.　What is suggested about Ms. Wagner?

　　(A)　She has written an article for the April issue of the magazine.

　　(B)　Her last article was favorably received by the readers.

　　(C)　She has to submit her manuscript by express mail.

3.　In which of the positions marked [1], [2], and [3] does the following sentence best belong?

　　"So, consider those things when you select the topic this time, too."

　　(A)　[1]

　　(B)　[2]

　　(C)　[3]

Questions 1-3 refer to the following text message chain.

Peter: 08:27 A.M.

Hi Lucy. I'm really sorry, but I just missed my train. I'm going to be late for the meeting.

Lucy: 08:30 A.M.

Really? OK. What time do you think you will arrive? Your presentation is due to start at 9:15.

Peter: 08:32 A.M.

The next train is at 9. I should be there at about 9:45.

Lucy: 08:35 A.M.

9:45? Wow. OK. I will pass it on to James. He is in charge of the meeting's schedule.

Peter: 08:40 A.M.

That would be great. Thanks so much.

Lucy: 08:45 A.M.

I just talked to James. He said you can begin at 9:50.

Peter: 8:47 A.M.

Great. Thanks. I managed to get an earlier train, the 8:45. I'm on it now. It's a faster one, too. It's due to arrive at Victoria Station in 30 minutes. I'll be at the office as soon as I can.

Lucy: 8:55 A.M.

Good. The meeting is just starting. See you soon.

Peter: 8:57 A.M.

OK. Thanks again.

---

1. **Why is Peter going to be late for the meeting?**

    (A) He wants some more time to finish preparing for it.

    (B) He missed his train.

    (C) He went to the wrong train station.

    (D) James didn't tell him about the schedule change.

2. **At 8:35, what does Lucy mean when she says "I will pass it on to James"?**

    (A) She will give the information to James.

    (B) She will let James give the presentation.

    (C) She does not think James will arrive on time either.

    (D) She thinks Peter should apologize to James.

3. **What time will Peter arrive at Victoria Station?**

    (A) 9:15

    (B) 9:30

    (C) 9:45

    (D) 10:00

Unit 7 関係詞

このユニットの文法事項では、関係詞を学習します。また、リスニングセクションではPART 3に関する頻出問題を解くことで頻出する問題パターンを確認します。リーディングセクションについては、PART 6形式の読解問題を通して、頻出する問題パターンや頻出語句を確認します。

Word Check

次の各語句の意味を下から選びましょう。

1. be involved in (　　)
2. primary (　　)
3. exhibition (　　)
4. lead to (　　)
5. complimentary (　　)
6. coordination (　　)
7. reimburse (　　)
8. refurbishment (　　)
9. various (　　)
10. suitably (　　)

(A) 払い戻す	(B) …に関わっている	(C) 無料の	(D) さまざまな　(E) 調整
(F) 適切に	(G) …に至る	(H) 主要な	(I) 展示会　(J) 改装

Grammar Section

■ 関係詞

1 関係代名詞

(1) 関係代名詞は、先行詞の種類と関係節の中での役割に応じて以下のように使い分ける。

先行詞	主格	所有格	目的格
人	who	whose	whom
物・動物	which	whose	which
人・物・動物	that	—	that

＊関係代名詞の目的格は、特に口語体（話し言葉）においては、しばしば省略される。

＊先行詞が最上級、序数、all、only、sameなどで限定されている場合、whichではなくthatが好んで用いられる。

(2) 関係代名詞を使った文と文のつなぎ方

(A) The agreement will be announced next week.

(B) We signed it yesterday.

① 2つの文の中で、同じものを指す言葉を探す。ここでは、agreementとitであり、agreementは先行詞になり、itは関係代名詞に置き換わる。

② itは物であり目的語であるため、itを目的格のwhichまたはthatにする。

③ 置き換えたwhichまたはthatを後者の文の先頭において、先行詞となるagreementの直後に後者の文を入れ込む。

→ The agreement *which*(*that*) we signed yesterday will be announced next week.

（3）関係代名詞の選択

《判別する方法》

● 関係代名詞の直後に、すぐに助動詞や動詞が続いている場合、主語の代わりをしているので主格の関係代名詞を選択する。

● 関係代名詞の後に主語＋動詞があり、先行詞とその主語の間に「～の…」という関係がある場合、所有格の代わりをしているので所有格の関係代名詞を選択する。

● 関係代名詞の後に主語＋動詞があり、先行詞がその動詞の目的語になる場合、目的語の代わりをしているので、目的格の関係代名詞を選択する。

例 題　（　　）内に入る最も適当なものを選んでみましょう。

1. Some of the officials (which / whom) we interviewed stated that they were involved in the project.

2. Our services are provided to inhabitants (who / whose) primary or home language is other than English.

3. We need to contact all the participants (who / whom) have already submitted their presentation file.

（4）特別な関係代名詞what

① whatはthe thing（s）whichに等しく、「～するもの、～すること」と訳し、主語・補語・目的語になる。

What she told us was not what we wanted to hear.

② whatの前には先行詞がなく、また、接続詞のthatとは異なり完全な文章は続かないことに注意。

（5）関係代名詞を含む熟語・慣用表現

① those who ～ 「～する人たち」

Those who want to apply for the new position should submit his/her CV and portfolio by the end of this month.

② what is called 「いわゆる」

Every employee in this section has got tired of deleting hundreds of what is called junk mail every day.

③ what is better / worse 「さらに良い／悪いことには」

We lost our way in the forest, and what was worse, it started to rain.

例 題　（　　）内に入る最も適当なものを選んでみましょう。

4. Some members of the division did not follow (that / what) the manager said this morning.

5. The exhibition application form will be sent to those (which / who) wish to display their work.

2 関係副詞

(1) 関係副詞の種類

関係副詞には次の4種類があり、先行詞の種類に応じて使い分ける。

先行詞	関係副詞	用 例
場 所	where	Lisa finally found the place *where* she could use free Wi-Fi.
時	when	Spring is the time *when* a lot of people visit this ancient city.
理 由	why	No one knew the reason *why* Mr. Martin had quit the job.
方 法	how	Ms. Lee complained about *how*（またはthe way）her boss had treated her.

＊the reasonとwhyが続く場合、いずれかがしばしば省略される。

＊the way とhowが続く場合、いずれかが必ず省略される。

(2) 関係副詞を使った文と文のつなぎ方

We booked the hotel.

We had stayed there before.

①関係代名詞の場合と同じように2つの文の中で同じものを指す表現を探す。ここではthe hotelとthereに注目する。

②副詞thereを関係副詞に置き換える。先行詞のthe hotelは場所なのでwhereにする。

③置き換えたwhereを後者の文の先頭において、the hotelの直後に後者の文を入れる。

We booked the hotel where we had stayed before.

3 関係代名詞whichの特殊な使い方

関係代名詞whichの先行詞が前の1語ではなく、前の部分や文章全体を受けることがある。

Mr. Chan achieved his sales goals for three months in succession, *which* led to his promotion to manager.

4 他に覚えておきたい重要表現

whatever「…するものは何でも」、whoever「…する人は誰でも」、

whichever「どちらの…でも」

| 例 題 | （　　）内に入る最も適当なものを選んでみましょう。

6. Any good salesperson knows well (who / how) sales figures can increase.

7. After entering your ID and password, click on JOIN HERE, (where / which) will allow you to access our database.

8. Mr. Franklin started his business with his wife in the year (which / when) they moved into the city.

9. Choose (however / whatever) you want to eat as long as it does not cost too much.

次の問題を解きましょう。

1. Mr. Harman owns three companies in Boston, (　　　) he was born and raised.

   (A) where　　　(B) when　　　(C) what　　　(D) on which

2. China Motors will demonstrate their new car (　　　) headlights automatically change color when it is in self-driving mode.

   (A) who　　　(B) which　　　(C) whose　　　(D) that

3. About half of the people (　　　) were interviewed said they were going on an international trip during this Christmas vacation season.

   (A) who　　　(B) whose　　　(C) whom　　　(D) which

4. This is a complimentary coupon to our customers (　　　) we have offered every Christmas for more than three years.

   (A) who　　　(B) whose　　　(C) whom　　　(D) which

5. Mr. Hassan's suggestion was fairly close to (　　　) we had planned to implement.

   (A) which　　　(B) that　　　(C) where　　　(D) what

6. 1966 is the year (　　　) the rock band came to Japan for the first and last time.

   (A) which　　　(B) whose .　　　(C) when　　　(D) what

7. A lot of users ask us (　　　) they need to upgrade their computer system at least once a decade.

   (A) who　　　(B) which　　　(C) the way　　　(D) the reason

8. This picture shows one of the rooms (　　　) we designed for a client in New York.

   (A) who　　　(B) which　　　(C) where　　　(D) what

9. After shopping or sight-seeing in Shanghai, you can relax in one of our bars (　　　) a complimentary drink will be served.

   (A) who　　　　　　　(C) where
   (B) which　　　　　　(D) what

10. Detailed direction will be given tomorrow by Michael Rogan, (　　　) is in charge of the event coordination.

    (A) who　　　　　　(C) which
    (B) whom　　　　　(D) that

このユニットのリスニングでは、PART 3の会話文について頻出するパターンの問題を解いてみましょう。PART 3の頻出問題としては、wantやask、suggestなどが入った問題が出題されます。その場合は主語になっている人物自身がヒントを言う可能性が高いので、はじめに問題文の主語が男性なのか女性なのかを確認しましょう。また、次の行動を問う問題は、会話の最後のセリフを聞き逃さないようにしましょう。

| 例 題 | 音声を聞いて、(A)～(D)のなかでどれが正しいか選んでみましょう。　🔊 Audio① 68-72
また、下にあるスクリプトの空欄には聞こえた語句を書いてみましょう。

Questions 1-3 refer to the following conversation.

1. What does the woman want to do?

　(A) Refund money

　(B) Reserve a table

　(C) Return an item

　(D) Buy a shirt

2. What does the man ask the woman to do?

　(A) Show him a proof of purchase

　(B) Call the repairperson

　(C) Present an identification card

　(D) Fill in a form

3. What will the man probably do next?

　(A) Direct the woman to the shirts section

　(B) Explain about the return policy

　(C) Return some money to the woman

　(D) Bring another shirt

《スクリプト》　🔊 Audio① 69

M: May I help you, madam?

W: Well, I'd like to ¹_____ this shirt. I bought it here last Friday, but it is a little ²_____ for me.

M: Oh, I see. Do you have the original ³_____ with you now? Our return policy says we cannot accept the return item without it.

W: Yes. Here it is.

M: OK. Then, which would you prefer, a full ⁴_____ or a ⁵_____ ? We have the shirt in larger sizes.

W: I'd like to be reimbursed, please.

練習問題 音声を聞いて、（A）〜（D）のなかでどれが正しいか選びましょう。　 🔊 Audio① 73-77

Questions 1-3 refer to the following conversation.

1. Why does the woman ask the man for help?

   (A) She spilt coffee over a document.
   (B) The copier is out of order.
   (C) She is too busy to eat lunch.
   (D) She has lost a car key.

2. When is the meeting scheduled?

   (A) At 10:00 A.M.
   (B) At 11:00 A.M.
   (C) At 1:00 P.M.
   (D) At 3:00 P.M.

3. What does the man suggest the woman do?

   (A) Call a repairperson
   (B) Go to work by bus
   (C) Change her password
   (D) Use another copier

このユニットのリーディングでは、PART 6の問題について頻出問題を解いてみましょう。
PART 6の頻出問題としては、重要英語構文や文法事項を問う問題などがあげられます。このユニットで学習した関係詞に関して、もう一度確認しましょう。

例題 次の文章を読み、空欄に入る最も適切な語句を選んでみましょう。

Questions 1-4 refer to the following advertisement.

New Updated Menu

Welcome to Curry King, the London curry restaurant made famous in the movie *Kana's Garden*. We are open again after a major refurbishment and we have a brand new menu, **-- 1. --** is even tastier than before. Take a look at some of the wonderful curries shown in the sample menu below. More details are available inside the restaurant. We are a perfect **-- 2. --** for singles, couples and groups. Groups larger than 5 can **-- 3. --** a free bottle of sparkling water. Step inside for a real taste of India!

Starters: Hot and spicy soups, Onion bhajis, Pakoras, Samosas - All at £10
Main course: Various chicken, seafood and vegetarian dishes - All at £25
Desserts: Various ice cream flavors available - All at £5
-- 4. --.

---

1. (A) whose
   (B) which
   (C) where

2. (A) venue
   (B) school
   (C) age

3. (A) make
   (B) give
   (C) receive

4. (A) Thank you for calling.
   (B) Our store is currently closed for cleaning.
   (C) All prices are before tax.

次の英文を読み、各空所に入る最も適切なものを選びましょう。

Questions 1-4 refer to the following e-mail.

To: spooners_petstore@spooners.com
Sender: jibterry@bmail.com

Dear Mr. Spooner,
I am writing to thank you for your advice you gave to my son **-- 1. --** pet food for his turtles. They seem to really enjoy the dried shrimp. I am wondering about buying a newer tank for **-- 2. --** for my son's birthday. As you were so helpful last time, I would like to come by your store and talk to you myself about a suitably priced one **-- 3. --** would fit into our apartment. Tom, my son, told me that your store is open on Saturday mornings, so I would like to come by this weekend and see you then. **-- 4. --**. I am looking forward to hearing from you.

Yours sincerely,
Terry Jib

1. (A) regarding
   (B) regards
   (C) to regard
   (D) regarded

2. (A) him
   (B) those
   (C) who
   (D) them

3. (A) who
   (B) that
   (C) what
   (D) whose

4. (A) I cannot say if it is possible or not.
   (B) Let me know if the order has been made.
   (C) Please let me know if this is convenient.
   (D) Send me a receipt as soon as possible.

Unit 8　仮定法

 PART 4　 PART 7

このユニットの文法事項では、仮定法を学習します。また、リスニングセクションではPART 4に関する頻出問題を解くことで頻出する問題パターンを確認します。リーディングセクションについては、PART 7形式の読解問題（ダブル・パッセージ、トリプル・パッセージ）を通して頻出する問題パターンや頻出語句を確認します。

Word Check

次の各語句の意味を下から選びましょう。

1. colleague（　　）　**2.** solid（　　）　**3.** statistics（　　）

4. generous（　　）　**5.** inquire（　　）　**6.** ship（　　）

7. process（　　）　**8.** replace（　　）　**9.** facility（　　）

10. accommodation（　　）

（A）宿泊施設　　（B）施設　　　（C）同僚　　（D）統計　　　（E）配送する
（F）処理する　　（G）取り替える　（H）寛大な　（Ｉ）しっかりした　（J）問い合わせる

Grammar Section

■ 仮定法

1 仮定法の基本

事実と異なることを仮定して話すときは、時制を一段階過去にする。

（1）仮定法過去

①現在の事実と異なるときには、過去時制を用いる。

I just wish I *lived* in New York now.

John wishes he *could* have enough time to prepare for the presentation.

②仮定法過去では、wasの代わりにしばしばwereが用いられる。

Everyone wishes he *were* here.

（2）仮定法過去完了

①過去の事実と異なるときには、過去完了形を用いる。

I just wished I *had lived* in New York then.

②法助動詞には、過去完了形がないため、「法助動詞の過去形 + 完了形（have + 過去分詞）」の形を用いる。

John wishes he *could have spoken* French more fluently then.

② ifを用いる仮定法の文

（1）ifを使う場合

①ifで始まる従属節を条件節（＝もし〜なら）、ifのない主節を帰結節（＝だろう）と特に呼ぶ。

②これらはいずれも事実と異なることを仮定して述べるので、仮定法を使って（時制を一段階過去にして）表す。

③また、帰結節は「〜だろう」と推量を述べる部分なので、法助動詞が含まれる。

If he *were* one of our clients, Ms. Bosh *would* never say such a thing.

The project *would have been* successful if he *had helped* us.

（2）「〜がなければ」のif構文

if it were not for 〜（仮定法過去）／if it had not been for 〜（仮定法過去完了）を用いる。

More banks *would* face serious consequences *if it were not for* governmental financial support.

If it had not been for the new medicine, the doctors *could not have saved* his life.

（3）実現性の低い未来の仮定

「万一〜するなら」のときは、were to 〜やshouldを使うことがある。

If he *were to* be promoted, many colleagues *would* be surprised.

（4）仮定法過去と仮定法過去完了の組み合わせ

「（過去に）〜していたら、（現在は）〜であろうに」というように、両者を同時に用いることもできる。

If it had not been for the accident, we *would* be in Osaka right now.

例 題　（　　）内に入る最も適当なものを選んでみましょう。

1. （ Should / Whether ） you have any concerns, please contact the front desk.

2. Ms. Caxton would have called you if she (weren't / hadn't been) busy.

3. If it (were not / had not been) for their financial support, we couldn't have achieved such a big market share.

3 ifを用いない仮定法と熟語・慣用表現

(1) 倒置

動詞／助動詞＋主語で始めると、ifを省略することができる。

Were I in your position, I would say the same thing in another way.

(2) without = but for

「〜がなかったら」の意味で、withoutやbut forを用いることができる。

Without Mr. Simon's advice, the negotiation would have reached a deadlock.

(3) suppose = supposing

ifの代わりに接続詞としてsupposeやsupposingを用いることがある。

Suppose (Supposing) you had one million dollars, what would you invest in?

(4) 仮定法とよく組み合わされる熟語・慣用表現

①even if ~: たとえ〜でも

Even if you were in my position, you couldn't lead this project to success.

②as if ~: まるで〜のように

Mr. Vincent always talked assertively as if he had been a judge.

③it is (high) time＋仮定法過去: もうとっくに〜する時間だ、〜してよいころだ

It is time (that) all the workers in this company enjoyed the same rights.

例 題 （　　）内に入る最も適当なものを選んでみましょう。

4. (If / But for) his constant guidance and solid support, we would not have been able to complete this research.

5. Kathleen would eat fast food (when / were) she very hungry.

6. (Even if / As if) it were not for global warming, we would need to build this seawall.

次の問題を解きましょう。

1. The statistics show that 65% of males wish they (   ) a little bit taller.

   (A) are   (B) were   (C) have been   (D) will be

2. If we (   ) at least 100 thousand dollars from investors, our business condition would improve.

   (A) secures   (C) are securing
   (B) will secure   (D) could secure

3. The trouble might have been prevented if the sales representative (   ) to the customer's complaint properly and promptly.

   (A) respond   (C) responded
   (B) will respond   (D) had responded

4. (   ) our manager's warning, we would have made a serious error.

   (A) Although   (B) As if   (C) But for   (D) Because

5. If you (   ) your computer last November or before, you would find its product number in the recall list now.

   (A) bought   (C) buy
   (B) had bought   (D) have bought

6. (   ) taken the exam, Mr. Johnson could have passed it with ease.

   (A) Were he   (B) If he is   (C) Is he   (D) Had he

7. Almost all of my colleagues treat Ms. Hume (   ) she were their boss.

   (A) as if   (B) even if   (C) if   (D) unless

8. It is about time we (   ) for our head office to make a presentation.

   (A) leaves   (B) left   (C) have left   (D) leaving

9. The exhibition would not have taken place (   ) Mr. Hendricks's generous and continuous support.

   (A) if   (B) unless   (C) with   (D) without

10. If Ms. Bright (   ) the report beforehand, she wouldn't have made such a mistake.

   (A) read   (C) had read
   (B) has read   (D) has been reading

Listening Section　PART 4　詳細な情報を問う問題

このユニットのリスニングでは、PART 4の説明文問題について詳細な情報を問う問題を解いてみましょう。詳細な情報については、問題文にキーワードが入っている場合が多いので、音声を聞く前に必ず問題文に目を通しておきましょう。

| 例 題 | 音声を聞いて、（A）〜（D）のなかでどれが正しいか選んでみましょう。また、下にあるスクリプトの空欄には聞こえた語句を書いてみましょう。 🔊 Audio① 78-82

Questions 1-3 refer to the following recorded message.

1. How has the speaker improved his vocabulary score?

   (A) By traveling abroad
   (B) By writing to Steve regularly
   (C) By taking a daily online word test
   (D) By listening to radio shows

2. What skill does the speaker think is the most difficult?

   (A) Vocabulary
   (B) Reading
   (C) Listening
   (D) Writing

3. Where does Steve currently live?

   (A) In England
   (B) In Japan
   (C) In America
   (D) In Jamaica

《スクリプト》　🔊 Audio① 79

Hi, Steve. This is Felix speaking. I just wanted to say ¹_____ for recommending that English learning website. It's really good. I've been taking the daily word test every morning on it since ²_____ _____ and my vocabulary score is slowly ³_____ ! I still think that ⁴_____ is the hardest skill to improve, so I'm going to start watching English ⁵_____ online. I'll check out some English ⁶_____ shows too. When you come back from the US, let's meet up. I can't wait to hear about your experiences ⁷_____ abroad. I hope to hear from you soon. Bye.

Questions 1-3 refer to the following announcement.

1. Who is the speaker?

   (A) A doctor
   (B) A flight attendant
   (C) A pilot
   (D) A fitness instructor

2. What has caused the delay?

   (A) Some mechanical trouble
   (B) The bad weather
   (C) A bad connecting flight
   (D) A human error

3. When will the flight most likely arrive at the destination?

   (A) At 10:00 A.M.
   (B) At 11:00 A.M.
   (C) At noon
   (D) At 12:30

このユニットのリーディングでは、PART 7のダブル・パッセージおよびトリプル・パッセージに関する問題について頻出問題を解いてみましょう。PART 7の複数文書の頻出問題としては、複数の文書の情報を組み合わせて解くクロスリファレンス問題や、書いてないものは何か（NOT）を問う問題などがあげられます。どちらについても文書の中で目を通していない箇所がないようにしましょう。

例題　次の文章を読んで、問いに答えてみましょう。

Questions 1-3 refer to the following e-mails.

To whom it may concern,

I'm writing to inquire about the order which I placed online last month. I ordered some books listed below and received the confirmation e-mail from your shop saying that the items would be shipped within a few days. However, the order has not arrived yet. Please let me know about the status of my order.

Titles of books:

1. The History of European Transportation
2. Italian Renaissance and Paintings
3. Tips on Traveling in Europe

Sincerely,
George Sanders

Dear Mr. Sanders,

Thank you for your e-mail about your order. We checked and found that your order has not been processed yet, because we have found that one of the books, which is on European art, is badly stained and needs to be replaced with a new copy. We are very sorry, but request that you wait a few more days before your order is shipped.

Sincerely,
Cindy Harper
GOOD BOOKS

1. **Why was the first e-mail written?**

   (A) To place an additional order

   (B) To inquire about the event

   (C) To ask for some explanation

2. **Which book is still not ready to be shipped?**

   (A) The History of European Transportation

   (B) Italian Renaissance and Paintings

   (C) Tips on Traveling in Europe

3. **In the second e-mail, the word "processed" in paragraph 1, line 2, is closest in meaning to**

   (A) opened

   (B) taken

   (C) prepared

Questions 1-5 refer to the following letter, flyer, and e-mail.

Dear Mr. Oman,

I hope this mail finds you well. I am very happy to inform you that your presentation proposal entitled 'Computers and AI in the workplace' has been accepted. We would like you to give your presentation at our conference in New York, in July of this year. Please send the conference fee of $150 via the conference website as soon as possible. Regarding accommodation for the conference, we recommend that you stay in a hotel close to the venue. I am attaching to this mail a flyer of one of the hotels that our conference speakers have used in the past. We look forward to seeing you in July.

Yours faithfully,
Lucy Garcia

MAPLE LEAF HOTEL

26, Isfield Road

Huntington, Long Island, New York

0124-262-128

Maple Leaf is located in the downtown area of Huntington in Long Island. In addition to our luxury pool and exercise facilities, we offer free taxi services to the nearest airports. Stepping outside the hotel, you can enjoy fantastic shopping and a variety of attractions for all ages. We have very reasonable rates and a variety of rooms to suit all visitors. We look forward to seeing you.

Double room	$150
Single room	$120
Family room	$180
Breakfast	$25

*All prices are per night.

Hey Jack, I just got a mail from Ms. Garcia regarding that conference in New York in July. She has asked me to send the conference fee. Can you do that for me, please? Also, she sent a flyer for one of the hotels near the venue. I had a look and I think it looks good. Can you reserve a single room with breakfast for 2 nights for me, please?

Please reply to this e-mail with confirmation. Thanks.

Robert Oman

1. **Why will Mr. Oman go to New York in July?**

   (A) To visit his family

   (B) To propose to his girlfriend

   (C) To present at a conference

   (D) To buy a property there

2. **What does Mr. Oman NOT ask Jack to do for him?**

   (A) Book a hotel room

   (B) Send a conference fee

   (C) Contact Lucy Garcia

   (D) Contact him again

3. **Which facility is NOT available at Maple Leaf Hotel?**

   (A) A swimming pool

   (B) Exercise facilities

   (C) Free transport to the airport

   (D) A four-star restaurant

4. **How much will Mr. Oman have to pay for his stay in the hotel?**

   (A) $240

   (B) $290

   (C) $300

   (D) $360

5. **In the flyer, the word "reasonable" in paragraph 1, line 4, is closest in meaning to**

   (A) affordable

   (B) diligent

   (C) negotiable

   (D) artificial

PART 1　 PART 6

TOEIC® L&Rテストでは、語彙問題が多く出題されるようになっています。このユニットでは、TOEIC® L&Rテストでよく用いられる語句を中心に学習しましょう！

Vocabulary Section　頻出する形容詞・副詞のフレーズ

次の各フレーズの空欄に入る最も適切な語句を、日本語を参考に下から選びましょう。

1.　an (　　　　) seminar　「集中セミナー」
2.　be (　　　　) priced　「手ごろな値段である」
3.　(　　　　) residents　「地域住民たち」
4.　a (　　　　) worker　「臨時の働き手」
5.　work (　　　　)　「残業する」
6.　at 3:00 P.M. (　　　　)　「3時ちょうどに」
7.　be (　　　　) prohibited　「固く禁止されている」
8.　the (　　　　) view　「そのすばらしい景色」
9.　be (　　　　) reviewed　「好ましく批評される」
10.　(　　　　) work experience　「これまでの仕事の経験」

(A) favorably　(B) moderately　(C) overtime　(D) splendid　(E) temporary
(F) previous　(G) local　(H) intensive　(I) precisely　(J) strictly

Question　次のうち、どちらが適切か選びましょう。

1.　Mr. Wilde is a really (efficient / spacious) salesperson.

2.　Please send this application (intentionally / quickly) because the deadline is soon.

3.　All of us are (grateful / helpful) for your kind advice.

4.　Our company has accomplished its sales goals for three (consecutive / enormous) years.

5.　The secretary (mistakenly / affordably) contacted another candidate for an interview.

以下の各英文の空所に入る最も適切なものを (A) ～ (D) から選びましょう。

1. It is ( ) that our company will be able to make a large profit for this quarter.

   (A) satisfied   (B) evident   (C) diligent   (D) direct

2. Ms. Lee ( ) opposed the hiring plan because it cost too much.

   (A) persistently   (C) numerically
   (B) accidentally   (D) deliciously

3. ( ) changes still need to be made to the agenda of the upcoming meeting.

   (A) Minor   (B) Illiterate   (C) Exhausted   (D) Enthralled

4. All the goods displayed on these shelves are ( ) from taxes.

   (A) requested   (B) appropriate   (C) exclusive   (D) exempt

5. The state-of-the-art smartphone which has ( ) been advertised on TV will be on the market this weekend.

   (A) anonymously   (B) recently   (C) usefully   (D) generously

6. To extend your contract, please send the enclosed form ( ) to us by the end of this month.

   (A) fluently   (C) prominently
   (B) significantly   (D) directly

7. It is ( ) that we complete the marketing research regarding our merchandise by next Friday.

   (A) delicate   (B) imperative   (C) wasteful   (D) informative

8. The ( ) two-day seminar on business manners will start from this Friday.

   (A) defective   (B) included   (C) competent   (D) intensive

9. Due to some mechanical trouble, the flight was delayed ( ) two hours.

   (A) ambitiously   (C) spaciously
   (B) casually   (D) approximately

10. This new lunch menu comes with a free drink for only a ( ) period of time.

   (A) limited   (B) fluent   (C) widespread   (D) costly

このユニットのリスニングでは、PART 1の写真問題について応用問題を解きましょう。

PART 1の応用問題としては、選択肢の中にbe動詞＋being＋過去分詞という「進行形の受動態」の文章が含まれているものや、または特殊な状況の写真や表現を用いたものがあります。いずれも熟語表現や特別な語句を知っていないと解けないものばかりですので、この機会に覚えておきましょう。

| 練習問題 | 音声を聞いて、(A)〜(D)のなかでどれが正しいか選びましょう。　🔊 Audio② 01-06

1. Ⓐ Ⓑ Ⓒ Ⓓ

2. Ⓐ Ⓑ Ⓒ Ⓓ

3. Ⓐ Ⓑ Ⓒ Ⓓ

4. Ⓐ Ⓑ Ⓒ Ⓓ

5. Ⓐ Ⓑ Ⓒ Ⓓ

このユニットのリーディングでは、PART 6の問題について応用問題を解きましょう。
PART 6の応用問題としては、文脈から解く語彙問題や、難易度の高い文法問題などがあげられます。
また、ビジネスの場面での定型表現などを用いた問題などは、事前によく使われる表現を覚えておく
ことが必要です。

練習問題1 次の英文を読み、各空所に入る最も適切なものを選びましょう。

Questions 1-4 refer to the following memo.

As -- **1.** -- in the last meeting, we have decided to embark on a new business venture next spring. To ensure the new business succeeds, we are planning to -- **2.** -- some experts in that field. If you know someone who is efficient and reliable, please recommend him or her to your division manager, Mr. Kramer. We will employ them in -- **3.** -- to other candidates. -- **4.** --.

1. (A) announce
   (B) announces
   (C) announcing
   (D) announced

2. (A) dismiss
   (B) operate
   (C) hire
   (D) apply

3. (A) supposition
   (B) preference
   (C) importance
   (D) response

4. (A) We are sorry for the inconvenience this accident may cause you.
   (B) We are going to clean the meeting room later today.
   (C) Thank you for your cooperation.
   (D) This will surely improve your manners.

練習問題2 次の英文を読み、各空所に入る最も適切なものを選びましょう。

Questions 1-4 refer to the following e-mail.

To whom it may concern,

I am writing this e-mail to -- **1.** -- about the periodical inspection of our factory scheduled for this Friday morning.

Mr. Sumner, our factory's foreman, has been absent from work with the flu since last Thursday. -- **2.** -- . However, it is unlikely that he will completely recover by this Friday. Thus, we'd greatly -- **3.** -- it if you could postpone the inspection for one month.

Please let me know if this sudden -- **4.** -- in schedule is possible.

Sincerely,
Catherine Loomba

1. (A) inquire
   (B) require
   (C) subscribe
   (D) maintain

2. (A) The hospital was very crowded with children yesterday.
   (B) Many orders have been placed through the Internet.
   (C) He is older than any of us by ten years.
   (D) Now he is slowly getting better.

3. (A) surprise
   (B) appreciate
   (C) estimate
   (D) restore

4. (A) criticism
   (B) change
   (C) chance
   (D) tradition

TOEIC® L&Rテストでは、イディオム問題が多く出題されるようになっています。このユニットでは、TOEIC® L&Rテストでよく用いられるイディオム表現を中心に学習しましょう！

▶ Vocabulary Section　頻出するイディオム

次の各イディオムの空欄に入る最も適切な語句を、日本語を参考に下から選びましょう。

1. (　　　　) into ~　　「…を調査する」

2. in (　　　　) with ~　　「…に従って」

3. (　　　　) to ~　　「…の前に」

4. at the (　　　　)　　「遅くとも」

5. on (　　　　) of ~　　「…を代表して」

6. (　　　　) a tax on ~　「…に税を課す」

7. aside (　　　　) ~　　「…は別として」

8. as (　　　　) ~　　「…に関しては」

9. in (　　　　) of ~　　「…の場合には」

10. be (　　　　) to ~　　「…に極めて重大である」

(A) latest	(B) case	(C) accordance	(D) behalf	(E) regards
(F) vital	(G) look	(H) impose	(I) prior	(J) from

Question　次のうち、どちらが適切か選んでみましょう。

1. This photocopier is currently out of (order / work).

2. We are planning to hold a retirement party in (action / honor) of Mr. Wilson.

3. We have to (hand / submit) in a report by this Friday.

4. Ms. Kerrigan will get in (attack / touch) with you this afternoon.

5. The new project is quite interesting in (respect / quantity) of its practicability.

以下の各英文の空所に入る最も適切なものを (A) ～ (D) から選びましょう。

1. The newly-released video game sells well since it can be enjoyed by everyone ( ) of age.

    (A) with regards
    (C) for the purpose
    (B) in response
    (D) regardless

2. We had no ( ) but to give up the project because of a budget deficit.

    (A) occasion (B) alternative (C) vacancy (D) value

3. What the division manager said in today's meeting will be acceptable ( ) our company's strategy.

    (A) in order to
    (C) in light of
    (B) as of
    (D) on his way to

4. ( ) an emergency such as fire or earthquake, be sure to evacuate from the back door of the building.

    (A) In accordance with
    (C) In spite of
    (B) In the event of
    (D) According to

5. ( ) that he wants to be promoted to manager, Mr. Ortega is lacking in some essential requirements.

    (A) Unless (B) Granted (C) Even though (D) Once

6. Naturally, our manager did not ( ) of the idea because of the high cost.

    (A) qualify (B) approve (C) generate (D) improve

7. As for the parcel which you sent us yesterday, it was ( ) to another section this afternoon.

    (A) recharged (B) included (C) forwarded (D) polished

8. The doctor advised that our skin should not be too ( ) to the sun in summer.

    (A) ridiculed (B) respected (C) exposed (D) forecasted

9. The orchestra concert that took ( ) last Saturday ended in a great success.

    (A) space (B) option (C) point (D) place

10. Mr. Cooke took the ( ) in embarking on the new project.

    (A) moment (B) initiative (C) limitation (D) occupation

このユニットのリスニングでは、PART 2の応答問題について応用問題を解きましょう。

PART 2の応用問題としては、問いかけに対してはっきり答えてくれないものや、定型表現で答えているものがあります。たとえば、Ask someone else, please. (「誰か他の人に聞いてください」)やProbably Mary knows about it. (「メアリーなら知っているかも」)、またSounds good to me. (「いいですね」)などの表現に注意しましょう。

|練習問題|　音声を聞いて、次の応答問題に答えましょう。　　　　　　　　🔊 Audio② 07-17

1.　Ⓐ　Ⓑ　Ⓒ　　　6.　Ⓐ　Ⓑ　Ⓒ

2.　Ⓐ　Ⓑ　Ⓒ　　　7.　Ⓐ　Ⓑ　Ⓒ

3.　Ⓐ　Ⓑ　Ⓒ　　　8.　Ⓐ　Ⓑ　Ⓒ

4.　Ⓐ　Ⓑ　Ⓒ　　　9.　Ⓐ　Ⓑ　Ⓒ

5.　Ⓐ　Ⓑ　Ⓒ　　10.　Ⓐ　Ⓑ　Ⓒ

このユニットのリーディングでは、PART 7の問題について応用問題を解きましょう。
PART 7の応用問題としては、文章のなかのキーワードから推測して解く問題などがあげられます。
また、複数の文書に関する問題は、幾つかの情報を組み合わせる問題も含まれているので、必ずすべての情報に目を通しておきましょう。

練習問題1 次の英文を読み、問題に答えましょう。

Questions 1-3 refer to the following letter.

Dear Mr. James,

Thank you for your review of my latest book, *Nature Regained*. I read it in this month's issue of *Modern Science Study*. It was very interesting. The point I wanted to make in my book was well summarized and explained quite clearly. On the whole, I am very satisfied with your review. However, there is one thing which I would like to correct you on. It is about the period during which I carried out the research. You wrote that it took place over two months, but actually it was over two years. I'm sure you will agree that this is a very significant error, so I would very much appreciate it if you would send a correction notice to the publisher at once.

Sincerely,
Norman Fisher

---

1. **What is suggested about *Nature Regained*?**

   (A) It was written by Mr. James.

   (B) It was reviewed in a magazine.

   (C) It is very interesting.

   (D) It deals with human nature.

2. **Why did Mr. Fisher write this letter?**

   (A) To invite Mr. James to dinner

   (B) To allow Mr. James to summarize his book

   (C) To thank Mr. James for helping his research

   (D) To ask Mr. James to correct an error

3. **Which of the following is NOT mentioned?**

   (A) Mr. James's review keeps to the point.

   (B) Generally, Mr. Fisher is pleased with the review.

   (C) The research conducted by Mr. Fisher was carried out over two years.

   (D) The publisher already knows the error in the review.

Questions 1-5 refer to the following announcement, letter, and letter of reference.

Abdel DIY and Home Improvements stores are now recruiting for our new Houston store. We have job openings in our sales and customer service departments and in the store warehouse. Those people applying for sales and customer service positions should have previous experience working in a busy sales environment. Applicants for the warehouse assistant positions should be warehouse safety certified. All applicants should send their resume attached to an e-mail to abdel_home@hiring.com. The closing date is June 26th. Successful applicants will be informed by e-mail at the beginning of July.

Dear Mr. Timms,

I hope this letter finds you well. As I am sure you remember, I recently moved to Houston to be with my family, after spending 10 years working in the warehouse at Timms in Dallas. I recently saw an online announcement for warehouse work at a new Abdel's that will be opening near me. I'll send you a link to the ad. I think that I have the experience required to apply to work there. Could you send a reference for me that I can attach with my resume, please? The deadline is June 26th.

Many thanks in advance,

Matt Wilson

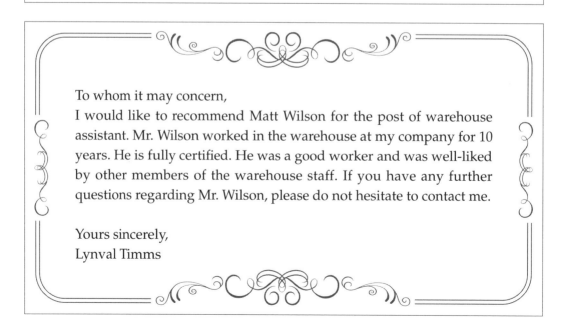

To whom it may concern,

I would like to recommend Matt Wilson for the post of warehouse assistant. Mr. Wilson worked in the warehouse at my company for 10 years. He is fully certified. He was a good worker and was well-liked by other members of the warehouse staff. If you have any further questions regarding Mr. Wilson, please do not hesitate to contact me.

Yours sincerely,
Lynval Timms

1. **What is the purpose of the announcement?**

   (A) To recruit staff for a new store
   (B) To invite presenters to talk about their goods
   (C) To offer discounts on a number of goods
   (D) To ask people for help in identifying shoplifters

2. **What should people wishing to work at the store do?**

   (A) Send their resume by post
   (B) Visit the store to arrange an interview
   (C) Attach their resume to an e-mail reply
   (D) Make sure that they send their resume before the end of July

3. **What warehouse experience does Mr. Wilson have?**

   (A) He does not have any experience.
   (B) He worked for 10 years in the warehouse at Timms.
   (C) He previously worked at another Abdel DIY and Home Improvements store.
   (D) He is currently working in the warehouse at Timms.

4. **What can be said about Lynval Timms?**

   (A) He is related to Mr. Wilson.
   (B) He used to work at Abdel DIY and Home Improvements.
   (C) Mr. Wilson used to be his boss.
   (D) He is the owner of his company.

5. **What does Mr. Timms's letter say about Mr. Wilson?**

   (A) Other members of staff did not like him.
   (B) He likes to answer questions.
   (C) He is going to start his own business.
   (D) He is a certified warehouse worker.

TOEIC® L&Rテストでは、語彙問題が多く出題されるようになっています。このユニットでは、TOEIC® L&Rテストでよく用いられる語句を中心に学習しましょう！

▶▶ Vocabulary Section 頻出する動詞・名詞のフレーズ

次の各フレーズの空欄に入る最も適切な語句を、日本語を参考に下から選びましょう。

1. improve (　　　　)　　　　　「生産性を向上させる」
2. (　　　　) parts into ~　　　「部品を組み立てる」
3. (　　　　) funds　　　　　　「資金を集める」
4. rapid (　　　　) in ~　　　　「…における急激な成長」
5. the (　　　　) of the company 「その会社の設立者」
6. (　　　　) the cost　　　　　「コストを見積もる」
7. fill (　　　　)　　　　　　　「処方箋に従って調剤する」
8. (　　　　) a product　　　　「製品を生産中止にする」
9. use (　　　　)　　　　　　　「注意する」
10. (　　　　) a new regulation 「新しい規則を実施する」

(A) raise	(B) growth	(C) prescriptions	(D) discontinue	(E) caution
(F) founder	(G) implement	(H) productivity	(I) assemble	(J) estimate

Question 次のうち、どちらが適切か選んでみましょう。

1. Mr. Hume often (visits / stays) in the hotel when he travels to Italy on business.

2. You need to show some (identification / operation) when you enter those facilities.

3. We are going to send you an (occupancy / invoice) of your order within this week.

4. MN Entertainment Co. is planning to (hold / mount) an audition for a movie.

5. The (warranty / renovation) period for the washing machine is 3 years from the date of purchase.

以下の各英文の空所に入る最も適切なものを (A) 〜 (D) から選びましょう。

1. Our environmental circumstances have been increasingly (   ) over the last decade.

   (A) reducing   (C) eliminating

   (B) deteriorating   (D) generating

2. Every employee including executives must (   ) the company safety rules.

   (A) comply   (C) donate

   (B) observe   (D) associate

3. The total number of attendees who (   ) in the event this year was 150.

   (A) attended   (C) intended

   (B) participated   (D) descended

4. Our president demanded that all of our department staff (   ) the problem immediately.

   (A) handle   (B) occur   (C) imitate   (D) deal

5. Some automobile companies in the district decided to make concerted (   ) to improve the local economy.

   (A) names   (B) efforts   (C) defects   (D) money

6. Last week Mr. Raw was (   ) by his immediate supervisor for his achievement.

   (A) declared   (C) founded

   (B) acclaimed   (D) limited

7. At our Taiwan branch, they (   ) three temporary workers last month.

   (A) entered   (B) boosted   (C) hired   (D) included

8. Our shop's annual sales campaign will (   ) throughout the week.

   (A) last   (B) ride   (C) present   (D) generate

9. Mr. Sasaki always tries to take some precautionary (   ) to deal with complaints from customers.

   (A) aims   (B) interests   (C) measures   (D) results

10. Light refreshments were (   ) to all the guests at the ceremony.

    (A) served   (B) removed   (C) sounded   (D) weighed

Listening Section PART 3 応用問題

このユニットのリスニングでは、PART 3のなかでも比較的難易度の高い「3人の間での会話」や「グラフや図表がついた会話」に関するものを扱います。3人の会話では、登場人物の名前が誰のものなのか、そして3人の関係などに注意しましょう。一方、グラフや図表などには音声を聞く前に数字や固有名詞に目を通しておいて、ある程度何が問われるのかを予想しておきましょう。

[練習問題] 音声を聞いて、次の問題に答えましょう。　　　　　　　　　　🔊 Audio② 18-22

Questions 1-3 refer to the following conversation with three speakers.

1. What most likely is the relationship between the woman and the men?

    (A) A shopper and sales representatives

    (B) Coworkers

    (C) A teacher and students

    (D) A nurse and doctors

2. Who is Mr. Norman?

    (A) A manager

    (B) A doctor

    (C) A designer

    (D) A musician

3. What does the woman say about the project?

    (A) It is very disappointing.

    (B) It is a secret matter.

    (C) It will cost too much.

    (D) It is hard to carry out.

Idea for reducing waste	Number of votes
Paper recycling	********
Less vending machines	*****
No paper cups and plates	***********
Recycling PET bottles	******

4. Look at the graphic. What was the least popular idea for reducing waste?

(A) Fewer vending machines
(B) No paper cups and plates
(C) Recycling PET bottles
(D) Paper recycling

5. When will the waste reduction be started?

(A) Today
(B) Tomorrow morning
(C) Two weeks from now
(D) In one week's time

6. What should the man do next?

(A) Send an e-mail to the woman
(B) Display some information in his section
(C) Reduce the number of workers in his section
(D) Think of some new ideas for reducing waste

このユニットのリーディングでは、PART 6の問題について応用問題を解きましょう。

PART 6の応用問題としては、前後の文章から解く時制問題や、難易度の高い語彙問題などがあげられます。また、接続副詞などの問題などは、事前によく使われる語句を覚えておくことが必要です。

練習問題 次の英文を読み、各空所に入る最も適切なものを選びましょう。

Questions 1-4 refer to the following notice.

As already announced in the last newsletter, the renovation of our company's parking lot -- **1.** -- on July 5. -- **2.** --. During the period, employees can park their cars at the space -- **3.** -- on the map attached to this e-mail. -- **4.** --, it is recommended that you use public transportation. By the time the construction starts, please tell your managers which option you will choose to take.

1. (A) started
   (B) starting
   (C) will be starting
   (D) had started

2. (A) The travel expenses will be reimbursed.
   (B) The manager will be transferred to another branch.
   (C) The work will be completed within two weeks.
   (D) A lot of people will visit the park this weekend.

3. (A) indicate
   (B) indicated
   (C) indicating
   (D) indicator

4. (A) Thus
   (B) In contrast
   (C) However
   (D) Likewise

Questions 5-8 refer to the following advertisement.

Adam Electronics has an exciting **-- 5.--** in our Tokyo office for a creative and experienced software engineer. We are an expanding computer software house and we offer an excellent working environment for ambitious, hard-working people. **-- 6.--** should have two years' working experience in the field and **-- 7.--** a Master's degree in computer science. They should be familiar with database management and program testing. **-- 8.--**. Make sure to send your resume as an attachment by e-mail to recruitment@adam.com.

5. (A) opportunity
   (B) computer
   (C) manager
   (D) problem

6. (A) Application
   (B) Applicants
   (C) Apply
   (D) Applicant

7. (A) at least
   (B) almost
   (C) nearly
   (D) maybe

8. (A) You can turn up at any time for an interview.
   (B) We will not be hiring until next year.
   (C) The salary is not so high.
   (D) They should also have excellent communication skills.

Unit 12　イディオム問題 2

 PART 4　 PART 7

TOEIC® L&Rテストでは、イディオム問題が多く出題されるようになっています。このユニットでは、TOEIC® L&Rテストでよく用いられるイディオム表現を中心に学習しましょう！

Vocabulary Section　頻出するイディオム

次の各イディオムの空欄に入る最も適切な語句を、日本語を参考に下から選びましょう。

1.　account (　　　　)　　　　　　「(割合を) 占める」
2.　(　　　　) with ~　　　　　　「…に従う」
3.　depending (　　　　) ~　　　「…次第で」
4.　(　　　　) repair　　　　　　「修理中で」
5.　on (　　　　) that ~　　　　「…という条件で」
6.　contribute much (　　　) ~　「…に大いに貢献する」
7.　make (　　　) for ~　　　　「…の埋め合わせをする」
8.　(　　　) with ~　　　　　　「…だけでなく」
9.　on one's (　　　)　　　　　「一人で」
10.　(　　　) to ~　　　　　　　「…に固執する」

(A) condition	(B) for	(C) comply	(D) up	(E) stick
(F) to	(G) on	(H) under	(I) own	(J) along

Question　次のうち、どちらが適切か選んでみましょう。

1. Mr. Ford is absent from the meeting today on (account / question) of his poor condition.

2. Surprisingly, his opinion (accorded / reminded) with mine completely.

3. We were very proud (from / of) our business expansion to other countries.

4. With (regard / intention) to the problem, we have to discuss a lot more.

5. Please refrain (into / from) smoking on the premises.

以下の各英文の空所に入る最も適切なものを (A) ～ (D) から選びましょう。

1. You can rest (   ) that your order will be shipped to your office in a few days.

   (A) resumed   (C) subsumed
   (B) assured   (D) covered

2. The marketing research team (   ) of seven members including our manager.

   (A) considers   (C) consists
   (B) consumes   (D) compromises

3. Ms. Saito is very (   ) to visit our factory in Kobe to inspect the new equipment.

   (A) formidable   (B) anxious   (C) engaged   (D) involved

4. (   ) completion of the lecture, Mr. Reed headed for the station to catch the last train.

   (A) Within   (B) Upon   (C) To   (D) During

5. Mr. Thomas was told by the president to take a 30-minute (   ) from work.

   (A) break   (B) relief   (C) belief   (D) motif

6. Generally, too much drinking or overeating can do (   ) to our health.

   (A) norm   (B) risk   (C) rest   (D) harm

7. Please note that visitors are (   ) from taking pictures in this museum.

   (A) included   (C) distributed
   (B) proceeded   (D) prohibited

8. Our company was named (   ) a famous local musician, Mr. Ottoman.

   (A) after   (B) into   (C) as   (D) throughout

9. Those (   ) in the training seminar are encouraged to sign up for it online in advance.

   (A) quoted   (C) interested
   (B) opposed   (D) satisfactory

10. Please remember that the plan is (   ) to change depending on the weather.

   (A) subject   (B) similar   (C) object   (D) familiar

このユニットのリスニングでは、PART 4の説明文問題について応用問題を解きましょう。PART 4の応用問題としては、文中の一文の意味を問うものや、グラフや表、または地図などの情報と組み合わせて解くものがあります。前者については、イディオムや定型表現が本文中では何を意味しているのかに気をつけましょう。また、後者については、音声を聞く前にグラフや表、地図に目を通しておきましょう。

| 練習問題 | 次のうち、どちらが適切か選びましょう。 | Audio② 27-31 |

Questions 1-3 refer to the following telephone message.

1. Where does the speaker work?

   (A) A storage company

   (B) A hotel

   (C) A refreshments company

   (D) A shipbuilding firm

2. Why does the speaker say, "Please confirm which room you would like to use"?

   (A) Their rental prices are different.

   (B) The rental price of a larger room will be reduced.

   (C) The services are different.

   (D) Another customer wants to use either of them.

3. What will the listener need to do next?

   (A) Send another e-mail to confirm the room

   (B) Reserve a larger room online

   (C) Change the number of cups needed

   (D) Call Ms. Bove

Jackson's Burgers Menu		
Burgers (all at $4)	Side-orders (all at $2)	Drinks (all at $2)
Regular Hamburger	Fries	Cola, Melon Soda
Double Cheeseburger	Salad	Coffee
Spicy Burger	Chicken Dippers	Milkshake

4. Why is Jackson's Burgers offering discounts?

(A) It is the wedding anniversary of the owner.

(B) It is the company's 10th birthday.

(C) The company wants to increase its market share.

(D) They want to celebrate the opening of the new store.

5. When will the St. James's Street store reopen?

(A) August

(B) June

(C) Next May

(D) July

6. Look at the graphic. How much will it cost to order 2 coffees, 2 fries and 2 Spicy Burgers during the offer period?

(A) $8

(B) $10

(C) $14

(D) $16

このユニットのリーディングでは、PART 7の応用問題を解きましょう。PART 7の応用問題としては、シングル・パッセージの「NOT問題」や、ダブル・パッセージやトリプル・パッセージなど複数の文書に関する問題などがあげられます。とくに、複数の文書の問題の中には必ず複数の文書を関連付けて解くものが入っていますので、その場合には、複数の文書の中でまだ目を通していない部分がないかどうか確かめることが大切です。

練習問題1 (シングル・パッセージ) 次の英文を読み、問題に答えましょう。

Questions 1-3 refer to the following advertisement.

Sales Representative Wanted

We at The Best Priced Items are currently seeking a sales representative who is willing to work for a branch which will be opening in Boston on October 20. Requirements are as follows:

- At least 3 years' experience in the same field
- Able to work five days a week, including Saturday and Sunday
- Exceptional skills in communicating with customers, both in person and over the phone

Remuneration and other benefits will be considered according to experience and ability. Successful candidates will be contacted by phone by our personnel director, Barry Smith, by September 30 to talk about the interview date. Those interested in the position should send a resume along with two letters of reference to the address of our headquarters no later than September 23. For more details, please visit our Web site!

---

1. What is the purpose of the advertisement?

   (A) To inform customers of an opening sale

   (B) To notify customers about the location of the new shop

   (C) To tell applicants about the date of an interview

   (D) To publicize a position vacancy

2. Which is NOT a requirement for the position?

   (A) Previous work experience in sales

   (B) Availability for weekends

   (C) Computer skills

   (D) An ability to deal with customers

3. By when should applicants send the necessary documents?

    (A) September 23

    (B) September 30

    (C) October 20

    (D) October 23

練習問題2 (ダブル・パッセージ)　次の英文を読み、問題に答えましょう。

Questions 1-5 refer to the following article and certificate.

CityRide bike scheme finally launches

On Monday, the City of Huntley launched its CityRide bike scheme, six months after it was originally scheduled to start. The scheme allows people to hire a CityRide bicycle for just £5 for 12 hours from any of the city's 600 CityRide docking stations. When they are finished with the bicycle, users simply need to park it back at any docking station. Payment is made when hiring the bicycle, either by credit card at a docking station terminal, or through the CityRide phone app. At the opening ceremony for the launch of the scheme, held at the Victoria docking station, Mayor Sajid Khan apologized for the delay of the launch of the scheme. Khan went on to praise the scheme, saying that it was "another wonderful green venture in Huntley." The CityRide bikes will keep track of their user's mileage. Repeated users who meet certain conditions will receive a certificate from Huntley's transport minister, thanking them for helping to protect the environment.

CityRide GREEN Certificate

City of Huntley
Awards you this certificate for completing 100km on a CityRide bicycle.
Thank you for helping to keep our city green.

Laurence Jones
Transport Minister
City of Huntley

1. **Where can users ride a CityRide bicycle from?**

   (A) All the parks in Huntley
   (B) One of 600 docking stations located in Huntley
   (C) Victoria's docking station only
   (D) 100 kilometers outside of Huntley

2. **How do users pay to use one of the CityRide bicycles?**

   (A) They can pay by cash or credit card.
   (B) They must visit the transport ministry and get a certificate.
   (C) They can use an app or pay by credit card.
   (D) They must pay only after completing 500 kilometers.

3. **Why did the mayor apologize?**

   (A) He was late for the opening of the scheme.
   (B) The scheme started later than was originally planned.
   (C) He didn't have the app installed on his phone, so he was unable to use a CityRide bicycle.
   (D) The spelling on the certificate was incorrect.

4. **How can users receive a certificate?**

   (A) If they pay by credit card or by using an app
   (B) When they have completed 100 kilometers on a CityRide bike
   (C) Every time they use one of the CityRide bicycles
   (D) After visiting each of the 600 CityRide docking stations

5. **In the article, the phrase "keep track of" in line 12, is closest in meaning to**

   (A) limit
   (B) remind
   (C) record
   (D) lose

基礎力確認テスト

試験時間 **40分**

このユニットでは、これまで学習してきた基本内容の確認をしながら、実際の受験の準備を行っていきます。できるだけ時間内に解き終えるようにしましょう。また、解答できなかった問題はよく復習をして、本番の試験に備えましょう。

PART 1 音声を聞いて写真を正しく表しているものを選びましょう。　　🔊 Audio② 36-38

1. Ⓐ Ⓑ Ⓒ Ⓓ

2. Ⓐ Ⓑ Ⓒ Ⓓ

PART 2 各問いかけに対して最も適切な応答を (A) 〜 (C) から選びましょう。　　🔊 Audio② 39-46

3. Ⓐ Ⓑ Ⓒ

4. Ⓐ Ⓑ Ⓒ

5. Ⓐ Ⓑ Ⓒ

6. Ⓐ Ⓑ Ⓒ

7. Ⓐ Ⓑ Ⓒ

8. Ⓐ Ⓑ Ⓒ

9. Ⓐ Ⓑ Ⓒ

Questions 10-12 refer to the following conversation.

10. Apart from learning to drive, what else did the woman do at the driving school?

    (A) She got a new car.

    (B) She made friends.

    (C) She got praise from her teacher.

    (D) She went camping.

11. Where is the man going to go in the afternoon?

    (A) To the driving school

    (B) To a car shop

    (C) To her friend's house

    (D) To the license center

12. Why can't the woman take the man to the driving school?

    (A) She doesn't have a car.

    (B) She doesn't have her license now.

    (C) She needs to take an intensive course.

    (D) She will get her license in two weeks.

Questions 13-15 refer to the following radio broadcast.

13. Who is speaking?

    (A) A famous actor

    (B) A radio presenter

    (C) A pilot

    (D) A film critic

14. Who is Judith Evans?

    (A) An actor who stars in the movie

    (B) A pilot who lived by herself on an island

    (C) The captain of a cargo ship

    (D) A film critic

15. Who most likely are the radio show's listeners?

    (A) People who want to be pilots

    (B) People who like movies

    (C) Captains of ships

    (D) Scientists researching about flying

16. Mr. James was ( ) by his supervisor to cancel the order placed yesterday.

    (A) request
    (B) requests
    (C) requested
    (D) requesting

17. We are very ( ) to announce the grand opening of our new store in this region.

    (A) please
    (B) pleases
    (C) pleased
    (D) pleasing

18. The trouble is that the guest ( ) has not arrived at the venue yet.

    (A) speaks
    (B) who spoken
    (C) is speaking
    (D) speaker

19. ( ) her stay in Italy, Ms. Joyce went to plenty of sightseeing spots including the Leaning Tower of Pisa.

    (A) Among
    (B) While
    (C) During
    (D) Though

20. Mr. Chan is a ( ) photographer who got an award last year.

    (A) pressed
    (B) promising
    (C) prolonged
    (D) preventive

21. As ( ) in the last meeting, our company is starting a new business related to advertising this month.

    (A) discuss
    (B) discussing
    (C) discussed
    (D) discussion

22. As soon as it ( ) raining, we will head for our client's office for the ongoing negotiation.

    (A) will stop
    (B) stop
    (C) stops
    (D) stopped

23. Mr. Atkins got his secretary ( ) a flight reservation for his business trip to London.

    (A) make
    (B) makes
    (C) to make
    (D) made

24. Ms. Lee ( ) the new plan because of the high costs and risks.

    (A) opposed
    (B) astonished
    (C) dedicated
    (D) interviewed

25. We have decided to postpone the (   ) monthly meeting scheduled for this afternoon until tomorrow.

   (A) regularly   (C) regularize
   (B) regularity   (D) regular

26. Mr. Luke succeeded in concluding the contract by (   ) after two months' negotiation with the supplier.

   (A) he   (C) him
   (B) his   (D) himself

27. The number of employees interested in the pension plan (   ) been increasing.

   (A) is   (C) has
   (B) are   (D) have

28. We ask you to recommend some staff members (   ) are willing to work over the weekend.

   (A) whose   (C) who
   (B) which   (D) what

PART 6 次の英文を読み、各空所に入る最も適切なものを選びましょう。

Questions 29-32 refer to the following advertisement.

A new sports bar is -- **29.** -- in Sanbancho Dori in December this year. The All-Star Bar will have lots of sports memorabilia, such as the baseball bat that Jiro Sato used in his last game and the sneakers -- **30.** -- by Mike Jolan during his time with the Sendai Spurs. The bar will be showing all the big sporting events each weekend, -- **31.** -- matches from the UK's Premier League, as well as golf, baseball and rugby. -- **32.** --. Contact Kai at 273-5537 for more details and prices. The bar is due to open next month but already has a website at allstarsanbancho.com. On the website you can find upcoming events information and food and drink menus.

29. (A) opening
    (B) opened
    (C) opens
    (D) open

30. (A) wear
    (B) wearing
    (C) wears
    (D) worn

31. (A) than

   (B) including

   (C) considering

   (D) where

32. (A) The bar will not be serving any food.

   (B) There is no parking available at their gym.

   (C) Dogs and other animals will not be included.

   (D) The venue can also be rented for private parties.

PART 7 次の各英文を読み、それぞれの問いに答えましょう。

Questions 33-35 refer to the following article.

Kysha's Records will be moving their London store to larger premises early next year. They will also be opening a second store in Brighton, in the southeast of England. The American-owned store has become very popular in recent years, thanks to their stubbornness to sell music on vinyl only. "More and more people are buying records instead of CDs or digitally now. They prefer the sound of music played on records. I do too, actually", said the owner and founder of the brand, Kysha Parks, from her Seattle home. The new London store will be twice the size of the old one. In addition, it will have many more records from an even larger variety of genres. The Brighton store, which will be opened by Parks herself next April, will be the same size as the current London store and will sell band merchandise, in addition to records.

33. What is the article about?

   (A) The hometown of the owner of the record store, Kysha Parks

   (B) The moving of a branch of a record store

   (C) How to import new records

   (D) Why CDs sound better than regular records

34. What will be different about the new London store?

   (A) It will be smaller than the Brighton store.

   (B) It will sell band merchandise as well as records.

   (C) It will be bigger than the current London store.

   (D) It will be moved from London to Seattle.

35. Which of the following is indicated in the article?

   (A) Ms. Parks prefers the sound of music on records to that of CDs.

   (B) People often complain that CDs are too expensive.

   (C) Ms. Parks says that CDs should be the same size as records.

   (D) CDs will no longer be sold at the stores in Seattle.

The 10th Anniversary of M's Kitchen, Established since 2010

We are proud to announce our 10th anniversary special price deal, available for this weekend only. This Saturday and Sunday, we will be offering our guests a 20% discount on our lunch menu. What's more, if you mention this advertisement, we will give you an original cup with our restaurant's logo printed on it!

Please come and taste our delicious food at reasonable prices. We are all looking forward to serving you soon.

----

*The number of our gift items is limited to 100 in total.

Special Anniversary Lunch Menu

- Ham and Cheese Sandwich with Drink
  (Coffee or Tea or Orange Juice) ··· $8.00
- Seafood Pasta with Soup or Salad ··· $15.00
- Vegetable Pizza with Drink
  (Coffee or Tea or Orange Juice) ··· $10.00
- Chef's Special ·· $20.00

*Pizza will be available on Sunday only.

To   : Kent Hamilton
From   : Cindy Radford
Date   : Wednesday, June 18
Subject : This weekend's schedule

Dear Kent,

Yesterday I saw an advertisement for M's Kitchen, a restaurant where we have eaten dinner together several times before. The advertisement mentions that it's the 10th anniversary of the restaurant this year. M's is very well-known for its lunches, such as hot sandwiches and their chef's Special and there's a special lunch menu this weekend with 20% off their regular prices. How about eating out for lunch there this weekend? If you can, I'd like to go on Sunday because they will serve my favorite food on that day.

Please let me know if you are available to go on that day by tomorrow night at the latest.

Best regards,
Cindy

36. **What is the purpose of the advertisement?**

(A) To announce the reopening of the restaurant

(B) To inform of a job opening at the restaurant

(C) To inquire about food prices

(D) To notify about a special deal

37. **According to the advertisement, what is suggested about M's Kitchen?**

(A) It has recently been relocated.

(B) It has opened its tenth branch.

(C) Its stock price is expected to rise by 20%.

(D) It will serve food at reduced prices for a limited time.

38. **Which of the following statements is true?**

(A) M's Kitchen started its business in 2008.

(B) Kent and Cindy have never visited the restaurant.

(C) The number of guests who can receive an item is limited.

(D) The restaurant is famous for its convenient location.

39. When will Cindy most likely hear from Kent?

    (A) Tuesday

    (B) Thursday

    (C) Friday

    (D) Saturday

40. What will Cindy probably eat at the restaurant?

    (A) Ham and Cheese Sandwich

    (B) Seafood Pasta

    (C) Vegetable Pizza

    (D) Chef's Special

このユニットでは、これまで学習してきた内容の確認をしながら、実際のテストの準備を行っていきます。できるだけ時間内に解き終えるようにしましょう。また、解答できなかった問題はよく復習をして、本番の試験に備えましょう。

PART 1 音声を聞いて写真を正しく表しているものを選びましょう。 📶 Audio② 55-57

1. Ⓐ Ⓑ Ⓒ Ⓓ

2. Ⓐ Ⓑ Ⓒ Ⓓ

PART 2 各問いかけに対して最も適切な応答を (A)〜(C) から選びましょう。 📶 Audio② 58-63

3. Ⓐ Ⓑ Ⓒ

4. Ⓐ Ⓑ Ⓒ

5. Ⓐ Ⓑ Ⓒ

6. Ⓐ Ⓑ Ⓒ

7. Ⓐ Ⓑ Ⓒ

Questions 8-10 refer to the following conversation.

8. What will the woman do tomorrow?

(A) Give a present to James
(B) Go to a meeting across town
(C) Go and see Steve
(D) Give a presentation

9. Why hasn't the man given the figures to the woman?

(A) His office is on the second floor.
(B) He is in a meeting.
(C) He has been busy.
(D) He had an argument with Steve.

10. What is the man going to do later?

(A) Go to a meeting
(B) Give a presentation
(C) Stay in his office
(D) Get some figures from Steve

Questions 11-13 refer to the following conversation and graphic. 🔊 Audio② 69-72

SCREEN		
Section A	Section D	Section G
Section B	Section E	Section H
Section C	Section F	Section I

11. Which show does the man buy a ticket for?

(A) 5 P.M.
(B) 7 P.M.
(C) 9 P.M.
(D) 11 P.M.

12. Look at the graphic. Which section did the man buy a ticket for?

(A) Section A
(B) Section E
(C) Section G
(D) Section H

13. What will happen after midnight?

(A) The concert will start.
(B) The parking lot will close.
(C) The customer will watch another movie.
(D) Customers can purchase tickets online.

Questions 14-16 refer to the following conversation with three speakers.

Audio② 73-76

14. **What is the conversation mainly about?**

(A) The upcoming company party

(B) A presentation meeting

(C) A new marketing research project

(D) The budget for a projector

15. **What does Jane imply when she says, "Actually, they looked really impressed"?**

(A) The projector was repaired.

(B) The marketing plan will be rejected.

(C) The plan will be approved.

(D) The board members didn't seem to understand the plan.

16. **What will the man do next?**

(A) Go out for lunch

(B) Prepare for his presentation

(C) Replace the projector

(D) Give a present to Miranda

PART 4 音声を聞いて、各問いに答えましょう。

Audio② 77-81

Questions 17-19 refer to the following excerpt from a meeting.

17. **Why are some members of staff absent from work?**

(A) They are on holiday.

(B) They are sick.

(C) They got a promotion.

(D) They don't want to work.

18. **According to the speaker, what will happen next week?**

(A) Staff will be transferred to another office.

(B) New software will be launched.

(C) Staff can all stay at home to relax.

(D) Staff will not be paid for overtime work.

19. **Why is the meeting taking place?**

(A) Staff are being asked to work overtime.

(B) All staff must have an influenza check-up.

(C) Staff are being asked to use public transport more often.

(D) The management have all been diagnosed with the flu.

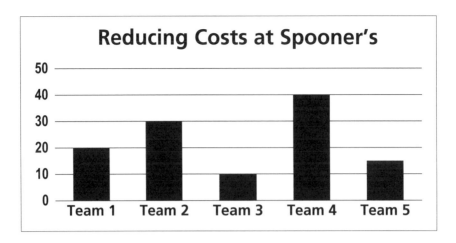

20. In what month did the program to reduce costs start?

(A) January

(B) October

(C) December

(D) June

21. Who was the leader of the winning team?

(A) Chet

(B) Hina

(C) Sinjay

(D) Laura

22. Look at the graphic. Which team will receive $100?

(A) Team 1

(B) Team 2

(C) Team 3

(D) Team 4

Questions 23-25 refer to the following advertisement. Audio② 86-89

23. What are the clothes sold at PCC made from?

    (A) Recycled clothes

    (B) Recycled plastic bottles

    (C) Recycled sneakers

    (D) Recycled wool

24. Where do the recycled bottles come from?

    (A) People who send them to PCC

    (B) The company's offices

    (C) City trash

    (D) Countries from all over the Earth

25. How can you watch the way PCC makes its clothes?

    (A) By buying clothes at their downtown store

    (B) By visiting their head office downtown

    (C) By sending them your old plastic bottles

    (D) By visiting their website

26. Please be sure to contact us (   ) to departing for your business trip.

(A) before   (C) prior

(B) including   (D) rather

27. Please avoid (   ) your cellphone on the train so as not to disturb other passengers.

(A) use   (C) used

(B) uses   (D) using

28. At Happy Prices, you will be able to purchase (   ) you want at reduced prices for the next three days.

(A) which   (C) where

(B) whatever   (D) in which

29. All of the division managers (   ) Mr. Williams attended the meeting last Friday.

(A) exclude   (C) excluding

(B) excludes   (D) excluded

30. The merger talks between AKB Drinks and New York Kitchen were (   ) by a famous lawyer, John Hume.

(A) occurred   (C) deserved

(B) involved   (D) mediated

31. Please send the invitation card for our new branch shop's opening ceremony to our (   ) customers next week.

(A) distributed   (C) prospective

(B) protective   (D) quantitative

32. The (   ) of the apartment will start at the beginning of next month.

(A) construct   (C) constructively

(B) constructive   (D) construction

33. We are worried about the harmful (   ) of smog on the human body.

(A) effects   (C) effectively

(B) effective   (D) more effective

34. During next week, employees are (   ) to use public transportation.

(A) encourage   (C) encouraging

(B) encourages   (D) encouraged

35. (   ) the talk, the author is scheduled to hold a book signing in front of the bookstore.

(A) While   (C) Following

(B) Even though   (D) Across from

PART 6 | 次の英文を読み、各空所に入る最も適切なものを選びましょう。

Questions 36-39 refer to the following memo.

Memo
To staff at all Deacon's PC Parts stores.
As you all -- **36.** --, our New Year special sale is due to start on January 2 next year. I know that you are very busy getting the stores ready for what, I am sure, will be a very busy period. -- **37.** --, there was an error on the flyers that were -- **38.** -- to shoppers during the Christmas period. The flyers state that customers can get 50% reduction on 4k PC monitors. -- **39.** --. If customers ask for the 50% reduction, please apologize and offer them a 10% discount on any other item in the store. Thanks for your cooperation.

Yours sincerely,
Joseph Deacon, Manager

36. (A) knows
     (B) know
     (C) known
     (D) knowing

37. (A) Unfortunately
     (B) Yes
     (C) Luckily
     (D) Maybe

38. (A) distribute
     (B) distribution
     (C) distributed
     (D) distributing

39. (A) We can all enjoy the holiday season.
     (B) Please go on to the next procedure.
     (C) We will be closed tomorrow.
     (D) They should have read 5%.

Questions 40-41 refer to the following text message.

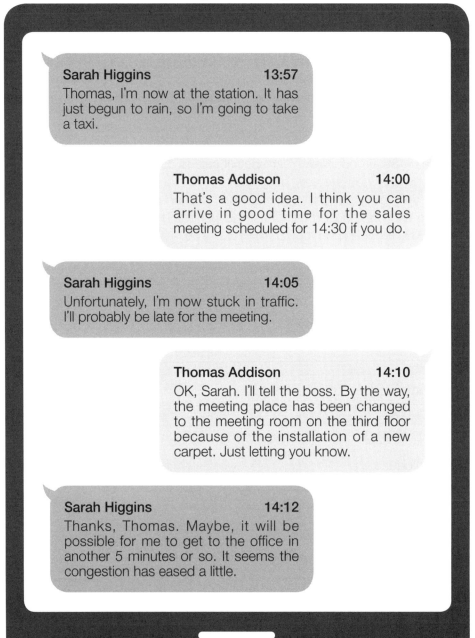

Sarah Higgins   13:57
Thomas, I'm now at the station. It has just begun to rain, so I'm going to take a taxi.

Thomas Addison   14:00
That's a good idea. I think you can arrive in good time for the sales meeting scheduled for 14:30 if you do.

Sarah Higgins   14:05
Unfortunately, I'm now stuck in traffic. I'll probably be late for the meeting.

Thomas Addison   14:10
OK, Sarah. I'll tell the boss. By the way, the meeting place has been changed to the meeting room on the third floor because of the installation of a new carpet. Just letting you know.

Sarah Higgins   14:12
Thanks, Thomas. Maybe, it will be possible for me to get to the office in another 5 minutes or so. It seems the congestion has eased a little.

40. At 14:10, what does Mr. Addison refer to when he writes, "Just letting you know"?

(A) The boss is angry with Ms. Higgins for her late return to the office.

(B) A certain change has been made to the meeting schedule.

(C) The ceiling of the meeting room is leaking because of the rain.

(D) The new carpet cost too much.

41. At 14:12, what does Ms. Higgins indicate?

    (A) She is now attending the sales meeting on behalf of the team.

    (B) She is worried about the weather condition.

    (C) She is likely to be in time for the meeting after all.

    (D) She is a taxi driver who recently joined the company.

Questions 42-45 refer to the following notice.

Tour of Europe's most interesting buildings

Calling all architecture and engineering students! This year, as in previous years, the department of civil engineering and the department of architecture here at PrimTech University are inviting its students to a tour of Europe. — [1] —. On the tour, participants will visit eight European cities and see some of the wonderful buildings there, learning about their historical and architectural importance. — [2] —. During the 10-day trip, students will also have the chance to practice their English skills as well as enjoy some wonderful European food and culture. — [3] —. Places are limited, so interested students should come to the student affairs section found on the main campus and register as soon as possible! There will be an explanation meeting on Friday September 3 at 5 P.M. — [4] —. Come and join us!

---

42. What is the purpose of the notice?

    (A) To inform students of a European tour

    (B) To ask students to pay money to build a European-style building

    (C) To encourage students to eat more European food

    (D) To get students to register for English classes

43. What is NOT one of the highlights of the tour mentioned?

    (A) Students can practice their English skills.

    (B) Students can enjoy some European food.

    (C) Students will visit eight cities.

    (D) Students can do a homestay with a European family.

44. What should students do if they want to join the tour?

    (A) Make sure their English skills are good enough

    (B) Register at the student affairs section at the university

    (C) Visit the civil engineering and architecture departments

    (D) Study about Europe's historical and architectural importance

45. In which of the positions marked [1], [2], [3] and [4] does the following sentence best belong?

    "You can get more details about the tour at that time."

    (A) [1]   (B) [2]   (C) [3]   (D) [4]

このユニットでは、さらなるスコアアップを目指して、リスニングセクションでは、PART 3とPART 4の問題、そしてリーディングセクションでは、PART 5、PART 6、PART 7について補強問題を用意しました。これまでの学習内容のまとめにもなりますので、しっかりと取り組んでください。

Listening Section

PART 3 音声を聞いて、各問いに答えましょう。　🔊 Audio② 90-93

Questions 1-3 refer to the following conversation.

1.　What was the news about Panda Lizard?

(A) They will release a new CD.

(B) They don't want to go on tour.

(C) They will break up soon.

(D) They have just finished a tour.

2.　Why does the man thank the woman?

(A) She got tickets online.

(B) His favorite band will break up.

(C) His friend sent him a link to see his favorite band.

(D) He was only able to get one ticket.

3.　What will the man do this evening?

(A) Watch a TV program

(B) Go to the movies

(C) Go to a fitness club

(D) Work overtime

PART 4 音声を聞いて、各問いに答えましょう。　🔊 Audio② 94-97

Questions 1-3 refer to the following radio advertisement.

1.　What kind of service is being advertised?

(A) Educational materials

(B) Website creation

(C) Internet access

(D) Computer repair

2. What kind of help can users get from CircleWeb?

(A) All year-round discounts

(B) A house visit from its support staff

(C) 24 hour phone support

(D) Online help at any time

3. What benefits will people receive if they sign up this week?

(A) A free catalog

(B) A mobile-friendly design

(C) Some tools to help create a website

(D) A discount

Reading Section

PART 5　次の各英文の空所に入る最も適切なものを選びましょう。

1. Ms. Anderson eventually got a job that is more (　　　　) than her previous one.

(A) lucrative　　　　　(C) financial

(B) binary　　　　　　(D) operative

2. Our boss's (　　　) into the world economy is trustworthy.

(A) insight　　　　　(C) installation

(B) reputation　　　(D) permission

3. To enhance the motivation of workers, offering them some (　　　) such as a bonus is effective.

(A) exemptions　　　(C) questions

(B) incentives　　　(D) nominations

4. The author's latest novel (　　　) me so much that I recommended it to my friends.

(A) returned　　　　(C) disappointed

(B) moved　　　　　(D) originated

5. This concert hall can (　　　) two thousand people.

(A) compile　　　　(C) ameliorate

(B) accommodate　(D) tailor

6. The food company (　　　) in 1869 suddenly went bankrupt last month.

(A) to establish　　(C) establishing

(B) established　　(D) has established

7. Today's sales were (   ) lower than usual.

(A) slightly   (C) conditionally
(B) fast   (D) punctually

8. Ms. Egerton was pleased with the news, (   ) her boss seemed dissatisfied with it.

(A) whereby   (C) until
(B) whereas   (D) without

9. Mr. Ray's diet is (   ) regulated by a nutritionist because of his diabetes.

(A) famously   (C) quickly
(B) strictly   (D) incidentally

10. Ms. Stow, our president, has been (   ) supporting activities by the charity organization.

(A) enthusiastically   (C) illegibly
(B) concisely   (D) automatically

11. Our division manager has (   ) bought a new smartphone.

(A) widely   (C) perpetually
(B) recently   (D) financially

12. We had our new computers (   ) to the office by the staff.

(A) carry   (C) carried
(B) carries   (D) carrying

13. (   ) you enter the room, you have to keep quiet.

(A) Whatever   (C) As if
(B) Once   (D) During

14. Our research members have many challenging problems to (   ) at present.

(A) reply   (C) address
(B) accord   (D) inhabit

15. The (   ) documents about our clients should be stored in a locked cabinet.

(A) confidential   (C) simultaneous
(B) edible   (D) zealous

Questions 1-4 refer to the following memorandum.

Memo
To: All management team members

Dear Staff,
In July, we will be holding our -- **1.** -- training session for all management team members. This year's talk will be on harassment in the workplace. As I am -- **2.** -- you are all aware, workplace harassment refers to actions or words that can cause discomfort or other -- **3.** -- feelings in the workplace. It is important that we are all aware of what harassment is and what we can do if we think we are being harassed. As always, during the training session, you will be given handouts and posters to distribute to your co-workers and display in your workplaces. Attendance at the training session is compulsory. -- **4.** --.

1. (A) annual
   (B) irregular
   (C) lazy
   (D) sometimes

2. (A) beware
   (B) awed
   (C) sure
   (D) known

3. (A) negate
   (B) negatively
   (C) negative
   (D) negation

4. (A) We look forward to seeing you there.
   (B) You do not have to attend if you do not want to.
   (C) It was great to see you.
   (D) Please don't forget to bring the posters with you.

PART 7

次の英文を読み、それぞれの問いに答えましょう。

Questions 1-4 refer to the following online chat discussion.

Chat room participants:

Jack Toom ················· Moderator
Emma Wang ················ Marketing manager
Trang Nguyen ············· Store manager
Stefan Domoney ········· Security manager
Lauren McCartney ······ Human resources

Jack:　OK. It looks like everyone is here in the chat room. Thanks for joining this online feedback session. What did you all think of the presentation for the new store?

Trang:　I thought it was great and I think the plan for the new store looks fantastic. I can't wait to get started.

Lauren:　I don't agree. I think it still needs a lot of planning. During the presentation, we didn't hear anything about how many staff we will need.

Stefan:　I agree with Lauren. In addition, I don't like the planned design of the store at all. I've never seen a yellow store front before.

Jack:　What about you, Emma?

Emma:　Actually, I think that the downtown area needs some new, exciting looking stores to make it look more modern. I thought the presentation was really dynamic.

Lauren:　When is the store due to open?

Jack:　Next January.

Stefan:　That doesn't give any of us much time to get ready.

Lauren:　Yes, Stefan is right. Emma, do you think we can be ready on time?

Emma:　I think so, but we all need to work together and help each other out if necessary.

Trang:　I agree.

Stefan:　I suppose so. I think I'm going to go and see the management after this and talk about my concerns.

Lauren:　I'll go with you, Stefan. I'm really not happy about this.

Jack:　OK. Let's end this meeting here. There will be another presentation next week on the same topic. Let's meet online again next week to talk about it. Thanks, everyone.

1. **What is everyone discussing?**

   (A) A presentation for a new store

   (B) What time they should meet next week

   (C) How they can improve online meetings

   (D) How they can recruit new workers

2. **What is planned to happen next January?**

   (A) The color will be changed.

   (B) The new store will open.

   (C) Stefan will go and see the management.

   (D) The next meeting will take place.

3. **What will happen next week?**

   (A) The participants will have another online meeting.

   (B) The new store will open.

   (C) Trang will begin work with Emma.

   (D) Lauren will go with Stefan to see the management.

4. **What does Emma suggest workers should do to get ready on time?**

   (A) Go and see the management

   (B) Try and do lots of planning

   (C) Work together

   (D) Cancel the next meeting

DEVELOP GRAMMATICAL COMPETENCE FOR THE TOEIC® L&R TEST
TOEIC® L&R テスト 文法項目別トレーニング

2020 年 4 月 10 日　初版第 1 刷発行
2023 年 4 月 5 日　初版第 4 刷発行

著　　者　鈴木　淳／高橋哲徳／高橋史朗／ Simon Cooke

発 行 者　森　信久
発 行 所　**株式会社　松 柏 社**
　　　　　〒 102-0072　東京都千代田区飯田橋 1 - 6 - 1
　　　　　TEL　03 (3230) 4813（代表）
　　　　　FAX　03 (3230) 4857
　　　　　http://www.shohakusha.com
　　　　　e-mail: info@shohakusha.com

装　　幀　小島トシノブ（NONdesign）
本文レイアウト・組版　中村亮平／品木雅美（有限会社ケークルーデザインワークス）
印刷・製本　日経印刷株式会社
ISBN978-4-88198-758-2
略号 = 758